TOWARD A CHICANO SOCIAL SCIENCE

TOWARD A CHICANO SOCIAL SCIENCE

IRENE I. BLEA

PRAEGER

Westport, Connecticut
London

Library of Congress Cataloging-in-Publication Data

Blea, Irene I. (Irene Isabel)
  Toward a Chicano social science / Irene I. Blea.

    p.   cm.
    Bibliography: p.
    ISBN 0-275-92408-4 (alk. paper)
    ISBN 0-275-92531-5 (pbk. : alk. paper)
    1. Mexican Americans—Social conditions.   2. United States—Social
conditions—1980-   I. Title.
E184.M5B57   1988
305.8'6872'073—dc19   88-6593

Library of Congress Catalog Card Number: 88-6593
ISBN: 0-275-92408-4
       0-275-92531-5 (pbk.)

First published in 1988

Praeger Publishers, 88 Post Road West, Westport, CT 06881
An imprint of Greenwood Publishing Group, Inc.

Printed in the United States of America

The paper used in this book complies with the
Permanent Paper Standard issued by the National
Information Standards Organization (Z39.48–1984).

P

Contents

Acknowledgments ix
Preface xi
Introduction xiii

1. Chicano Studies and the Social Sciences 1

Introduction 1
A Suppressed History 1
A Review of Community Studies 4
Academic Impacts on Chicano Studies 6
Early Research on Chicanos by Chicanos 8
Updating the Social Sciences 11
The Function of Sociological Theory 13
Accepting the Mirande Challenge 15
The Role of Discrimination 17
The Internal Colonial Model 18
A Review of Chicano Social History 21
Summary 24
References 25

2. Social Stratification by Race, Class, and Gender 29

Introduction	29
The Impact of Social Stratification	29
Social Deviance Theory and Stratification	31
Social Stratification and the Ideology of Liberation	32
The Study of Social Exclusion	36
Chicanos and the Class Structure	37
Sexism in Society	39
Chicana Cultural Importance	40
Multi-Segmented Social System	42
Summary	44
References	44

3. Social-Cultural Profile 47

Introduction	47
The Role of Religion	48
Marriage and Female-Male Relationships	50
Negative Gender Relationships	51
Significant Cultural Observances	55
Cultural Values	58
The Role of Ethnicity	59
Summary	63
References	65

4. Mexican American Female Experience 67

Introduction	67
Third World Women	68
Feminist Conflict in the Chicano Movement	71
A Review of Chicana History	72
Chicanas North of Mexico	77
Social Stratification in Academe	82
Contemporary Chicana Feminist Issues	86
Summary	88
References	89

5. Social Control and the Chicano Experience 91

Introduction 91
Chicano Society 92
Social Deviance and the Chicano Community 92
Collective Behavior and a Model of Resistance 97
Decolonization as a Model for Social Change 103
The Language of Social Change 108
Summary 111
References 112

6. Electoral and Nonelectoral Politics 115

Introduction 115
Two Kinds of Politics 116
The Chicano Movement 118
Electoral Politics 121
Recent Electoral Politics 122
The Current Strategy 125
A Multifaceted Approach to Addressing Issues 129
The Next Generation 130
Summary 134
References 136

7. Toward a Renewed Social Science 139

Introduction 139
Acknowledging the Contribution 140
The Internal Colonial Model Reviewed 141
The Politics of Social Science 144
Realigning the Social Sciences 145
Reviewing the Discrimination Cycle 146
Summary 149
Reference 150

Selected Bibliography 151
Index 155
About the Author 161

Acknowledgments

A special embrace and thank you go to my daughter, Regina Rene Gutiérrez, 21 years old, who managed our household during the time I was writing. Also appreciated is my student, Marlene, who helped with the typing; Dan, who listened to my ideas; and my special friends Nancy, Tony, and Jay, who taught me word processing over the telephone.

Preface

The most significant population in the United States is its Hispanic population. The largest group of that population is known as Chicano. Basically, it is composed of a smaller and relatively new middle class, usually referred to as bureaucrats, and a much larger group of people, usually referred to as grass roots.

An excellent example of the two segments working together is the National Hispanic Agenda. On October 19–21, 1987, representatives from various Latino groups met in Washington, D.C., to formulate a course of empowerment for Hispanics. Various proposals were made, but leading the plan were the following three demands to be made of the candidates and the winner of the 1988 presidential election: The candidates for the office, and the new president, must take a position against the "English as the official language of the United States" movement; there must be a Hispanic appointed to the president's cabinet; and the importance of bilingual education must be maintained.

The importance of diplomatic relations is stressed in the agenda. In fact, many public speakers are noting that the U.S. Spanish-speaking population can act as a bridge to better diplomatic relationships with other Spanish-speaking countries. The goal of this book is to inform the reader about the Chicano population and its concerns.

Introduction

A book on the nation's largest minority group is timely because of the potential impact of the group on America's future. The large number of Chicanos will affect national, state, and city elections; business; the nature of education; foreign policy; medical practices; art; music; and how American citizens relate to persons of color.

The population's impact is particularly felt in the schools, where, in many large cities, racial and ethnic minorities constitute the majority of the population. The need for retraining of teachers and administrators is immediate. Those who know how to teach and design policy relevant to Hispanic children are few. The need for qualified individuals is also being felt in the social services and medicine. Primarily the need is to understand the Chicano in order not only to be able to provide services but also to better race and ethnic relations in the United States.

This book presents an overview of the nature and character of Mexican Americans in the United States. It surveys their culture, their values, and their major social institutions and how they function in a minority status relationship to the dominant, Anglo society. Focus will be upon coping mechanisms and upon the creativity and sustaining power of a culture under constant attack.

A feminist perspective is incorporated into this book, a perspective that is severely lacking in most work on Chicanos. It does this to present more fully and accurately a life-style that values gender differences as a means of survival, and to acknowledge the contributions of Chicana feminists to the study of Chicanos.

This book reviews family life, the life of men and women and children. It looks at the elements of social control, social stratification, politics, education, religion, and how the population has been studied in the social sciences.

The strong sociological perspective of this book is representative of the author's training. It also represents the author's 12-year experience teaching Chicano studies at the university and college level. In this text two disciplines have been combined to illustrate the demand for an interdisciplinary approach to the study of some elements of the Chicano existence.

The author uses the term "Chicano" with full awareness of the fact that to some it is still an offensive term connoting critical and radical politics. However, other terms are used to refer to the population. "Hispanic" is, generally, used in the generic sense, and includes Spanish-speaking people from various countries. "Mexican American" and "Chicano" refer to persons of Mexican ancestry living in the United States.

Of primary interest is students. This book is written as a textbook to assist in the teaching and learning of students. It is written with all students in mind. It is also written with teachers in mind. Students will find the book valuable because it presents material taught minimally, if at all, in public schools. This will assist Chicano students in learning about themselves. Non-Chicano students will learn not only what they are not learning in traditional classrooms but also about themselves and their country, and will be in a better position to select the quality of their future.

In this book the realigning of the educational curriculum and the social stratification system in the United States is advocated. Of special concern is racial and gender stratification. It is felt that racism and sexism have stalemated American culture and harnessed American social science, thereby keeping it from making a world contribution. With the elimination of racism and sexism, America will be able to practice and grow from a diversity of cultures, and the social sciences will emerge, claiming the newest advances in scholarship.

This book is not written with malice, animosity, rancor, or scorn. It is written with admiration, respect, and appreciation of cultural diversity. It is written in the hope of motivating further research, writing, and improved race, ethnic, and gender relations.

1
Chicano Studies and the Social Sciences

INTRODUCTION

The study of Chicanos is relatively new even though the descendants of the Spanish conquistadores have lived in this hemisphere for over 400 years. Until the 1960s Chicanos appear to have lived peacefully with the dominant Anglo society. This appearance is deceiving, however; for about two centuries the two groups lived side by side with both latent and blatant hostility.

It also appears that nothing was ever said or done about the hostility. Many people feel there was no real basis for the hostility—if, indeed, it existed. There was no public documentation. There was no public knowledge. Again, appearances are deceiving, for much has been said and much has been done; but knowledge of this activity has been suppressed. The following pages will reveal briefly how this was done.

A SUPPRESSED HISTORY

In 1848 the Treaty of Guadalupe Hidalgo brought an end to the U.S. war with Mexico and created some 60,000 to 80,000 Mexican Americans (Chicanos). Some estimated the number to have been as high as 350,000. The war had been a bitter conflict characterized by racism and hatred on both sides. At the end of the war, former

Mexicans became subject to an American way of life that was foreign. It was also extremely oppressive.

The study of this phenomenon is, to a great degree, one of struggle and conflict; but the war did not create the conflict. It existed prior to 1848 and is rooted in the development of the United States as a country.

The American expansionist mentality was manifested in reactions to the conditions the Mexican government set up in order to allow Americans to live in northern Mexico. Mexico agreed to such an arrangement because it had few people living in the north. Americans failed to comply with the conditions and plotted war against Mexico. Part of the plot was to annex Mexico's northern territory and build a capitalist economy (Acuna 1981).

As time passed, conflicts over Mexico's conditions continued. The conflicts became physically and linguistically violent. Chicanos were called "greasers" and Anglos were called "gringos." War was declared, and after the fighting Mexico lost its northern territory. Mexico accepted the Rio Grande as the southern border of Texas and ceded the present states of California, New Mexico and Nevada, and parts of Colorado, Arizona, and Utah. It cost the United States $15 million to acquire the region.

After the war, there existed a dual economy with a dual wage system (Barrera 1979). Chicanos were excluded from education or their education was inferior to that received by the Anglos. Political participation was impossible. The Chicanos suffered religious discrimination. There were shootings, hangings, and general violence. It was not until the birth of the Chicano movement that Chicanos were able to present their side of the story to the American public. This was not a peaceful process, and in communities and campuses across the nation the struggle to keep the Chicano perspective alive continues.

The perspective sought to incorporate into public knowledge the fact that Mexico was thrust into an unjust war for imperialist reasons; that Mexicans had been discriminated against in the most violent ways. The Chicanos sought education as a way not only to relate but also to upgrade the Chicano experience. This perspective and Chicano attempts to implement social change were met with extreme resistance and more violence.

The Chicano people, however, persevered. They continued to address these issues. Many men, women, and children died. The apparent silence ended; and the Catholic Church and American education, politics, health systems, and economics were severely criticized. There were strikes, boycotts, marches, speeches, and sit-ins that kept the media busy.

The Chicano movement continues. Members of the reform movement work within the dominant system to promote social change and to upgrade the Chicano condition. Former activists are now attorneys, politicians, doctors, professors and clergy who help other Chicanos.

The conflicts also continue. However, the strikes, boycotts, marches, speeches, and sit-ins are more reserved. The media hardly respond. Chicanos demonstrating and complaining are old news. The most important strategy is to teach: to teach the Chicano perspective.

Early scholarly work on Chicanos is historical and political. Much literary work also has been produced. The concentration on politics and history is greatly attributable to the fact that men were the first to engage in academic scholarship. These men were students, then professors writing in their fields, which tended to be history and political science. They documented what was outstanding or out of the ordinary. This approach gave a limited view of what was important to Chicanos. It was not until sociologists and women entered the field that a more rounded, holistic perspective appeared.

This approach extended a feminist analysis and focused upon the everyday life of a minority in a dominant society. Areas of study include family structure, roles, rites of passage, the nature of work, female-male relationships, and female participation in economics, political organization, religion, and health.

In traditional academe, studies on Chicanos have focused primarily on race relations. Much of this work has been descriptive, concentrating on the poverty-producing factors of discrimination. While this has been a worthwhile endeavor, the strong presence of the population in the United States warrants a sociological analysis that goes beyond the study of the impact of discrimination and lends insight into how members of the largest ethnic group function in two cultures. Such a focus should begin by reviewing the function of the Chicano community in American society.

Chicano studies is an interdisciplinary approach to the study of the Mexican American (Chicano) experience in the United States. It has incorporated sociology, anthropology, economics, psychology, and the humanities. It accesses its analysis in a historical manner that traces social change and the impact of change upon Chicanos. But Chicano studies needs to go further. This means that the study of Chicanos has to be presented in a multifaceted manner that includes a view of the family, religion, cultural traditions, and gender and racial oppression. This calls for the use of sociology, which studies how institutions function in society, in general and in specific communities.

A REVIEW OF COMMUNITY STUDIES

In the study of communities, not much has been added since Robert Nisbet (1962) maintained that modern society has become so complicated and impersonal that it has caused alienation among its members. In its largeness, society no longer adequately meets human needs and has, in fact, produced an endless search for a feeling of belonging. In an attempt to counteract what the modern state has produced, Nisbet suggests the construction of small, cohesive communities.

Community is defined here as a unit of social and geographic organization from which emerge feelings of belonging through a network of kinship, friends, and acquaintances who share a common experience. This definition is used with full knowledge that much of America no longer lives in this manner. Chicanos do, however, and references to community shall also be in the larger sense of Mexican American society. On a smaller scale, reference will be extended to residential areas in which people live, play, and die. In this community people rest, make their homes, earn incomes, and rear children. This definition includes the totality of social interaction.

Since the 1920s there have been many sociological community studies. Dennis Poplin (1972) contends that there are several types of community research. Predominant are ethnographic studies, social stratification studies, and studies on race relations. These all focus upon the structure and dynamics of community and seek to answer the question, What is life like, and how is it organized? Poplin believes that these three types of studies are representative of community studies as a whole because they seek to understand the community in its totality.

One of the best-known examples of an ethnographic study is Robert S. and Helen M. Lynd's *Middletown* (1929). The Lynds sought to understand the life-style of middle America in an Indiana city. They concluded that American life proceeds upon the following activities: getting a living, making a home, training the young, leisure time and activities, practicing religion, and engaging in community activities. From the study there emerges a sense of what it was like to be middle class in America during the era of prohibition and prior to the Great Depression. Another insightful study is James West's (1945) research on a small farm community in Missouri. Plainville is an interesting rural contrast to Middletown and is still within an ethnographic approach.

Between 1928 and 1967, there were important ethnographic studies that focused upon communities within a larger community. Poplin refers to these as subcommunities. The term "subcommunities" will not be used in this body of work because the prefix, "sub," to most English-speaking Americans, implies not only smaller but also less in value (than the dominant community). A look at these studies does, however, give our endeavor somewhat of a historical perspective on ethnic community studies.

The first to appear was Louis Wirth's *The Ghetto* (1928), an in-depth look at blacks in an urban setting. After Wirth's study Herbert J. Gans published his Park Forest study (1962). Gans's work was preceded by Williams Foote Whyte's famous study, *Street Corner Society* (1955), on Italian males in Boston. In 1967, Elliot Leibow published the classic *Talley's Corner,* a study of black male street life. From this brief mention it is apparent that sociology has a rich history of descriptive studies focusing upon ethnic and racial minority communities. These community studies were heavily influenced by the Chicago school of thought. Sociologists, however, can extend their studies to include updated perspectives and analysis of the long over-looked Chicano barrio. Sociology can more fully present what happens within Chicano communities, how the dominant society affects them, what people create, and what keeps them culturally intact, in spite of overwhelming pressure to assimilate.

The history of sociology's focus upon the community does not end with ethnographic studies, however; Poplin contends that a second, earlier emphasis was placed upon social stratification at a local level. The best-known of these studies, by the social anthropologist W. Lloyd Warner and Paul Lunt, is *Yankee City* (1941). The most striking feature of this, and of all Warner's studies, is exploration of the class system.

To Warner's social stratification studies can be added August Hollingshead's *Elmtown's Youth* (1949), which found variances within classes in the same community. Expanding upon Hollingshead's work, Arthur Vidich and Joseph Bensman (1958) recognized that groups of approximately equal social standing differed from one another in values and beliefs. These works are of interest to those conducting barrio studies, for there are class differences within the structures of many barrios across the nation. Not all Chicanos are poor, and not all Chicanos of the same income group believe and act the same. There are regional, country of origin, and historical differences.

Somewhat consistent, yet different from the social stratification studies, are the race relations studies. These studies are more holistic attempts. They focus upon class but make clear the concept of race or caste—for instance, John Dollard's *Caste and Class in a Southern Town* (1937) and Allison Davis' *Deep South* (1941). In these studies the authors give insight into the social mechanisms that produce subordinate and dominant relations between blacks and whites in the South. Poplin omitted from his analysis the very important discussion of caste, which is founded upon a system of sentiments that both blacks and whites hold about themselves and about one another. According to Davis, the black rural caste system was organized around the control of sex. White males had easy access to black females, but white females did not have access to black males. In addition, the black population was relegated to a lower-class and lower-caste position based on color. Blacks could not climb out of a color caste social position. They could not escape the fact that their skin was black and that they were discriminated against because of that.

To test the concept of caste in an urban setting, W. Lloyd Warner assisted in directing the work of Drake and Cayton that was published as *Black Metropolis* (1945), a study of black life in Chicago. Unlike *Deep South,* this study did not provide insight into the white population. Drake and Cayton's emphasis is on economics, politics, migration, and class stratification: upper, middle, and lower classes. Their study concludes that caste also exists in the city.

ACADEMIC IMPACTS ON CHICANO STUDIES

The caste analysis has been extended to Chicanos, but there has been difficulty because the concept of caste in the United States is characterized by endogamy (prohibition of marriage outside the caste group) and by rigid racial, not religious, barriers. Mario Barrera (1979) cites a severe limitation of the caste school of thought when analyzing the Chicano. Not only is caste a concept closely identified with social conditions in India, where the basis is religious and not racial or ethnic, and, unlike the Chicanos, members of the society accept the structure and do not have it imposed on them by outsiders. In the Chicano experience the basis of racial-ethnic division is biological and cultural. Another definitional problem with the use of caste as a concept to understand racial divisions is that it lacks historical continuity. Historical continuity, the function of discrimination over time, is perhaps the largest contribution made by minority scholars and scholars of race relations to the social sciences and the study of discrimination.

Not until the 1960s did social scientists begin seriously to develop theoretical concepts that would lead to better understanding of racial and ethnic communities. Poplin omitted several of the community studies that emerged in the 1960s that were influenced by the Chicago model of community studies. The Chicago model and the War on Poverty influenced the work of David Schulz (1969). In an ethnographic tradition, Schulz paid close attention to black urban ghetto life in the heart of St. Louis. His work on growing up black in a housing project discussed the life cycle, birth through old age, of incomplete and complete families. There are problems with Schulz's family categories, however. His male and cultural biases imply that complete nuclear families are more legitimate and that incomplete (single-parent-headed) families are not really families. Schulz also focuses upon what is most deviant from mainstream Anglo society and, thus, has a tendency to view black urban life as deviant. The subject categories upon which he concentrates, however, are of great interest because he begins to take an institutional approach. This approach includes racial discrimination and how it deters attainment of employment, quality housing, and upward mobility.

With the exception of a few isolated studies, Chicanos were hardly studied until the 1960s. Two very early studies are Ruth Tuck's *Not with the Fist* (1946) and Lyle Saunder's *Cultural Differences in Medical Care of the Spanish-Speaking People in the Southwest* (1954). These and other studies on Mexican Americans are not truly community studies; instead, they fall into a category described by Poplin as "the community as an independent variable."

These studies treat the community as an influencing factor. Social scientists are more interested in the dependent variable, the impact of the community upon a specific entity such as medical care, than in a community way of life. The assumption of these studies is that a change in one variable (the community) causes a change in another (medical care, for example). Thus, in some early research, community size influenced fertility, attitudes, and values. These studies do not shed much light on everyday life, but they assist in understanding some community change and dominant social science tendencies.

In studies in which researchers have concentrated upon Mexican Americans, the ethnicity of the community becomes the independent variable. This sets the Chicano up as target for "blaming the victim" academic perspectives that do not take into consideration social forces such as class, race, and gender prejudice and discrimination. In "blaming the victim" approaches, the victimized—the community—is blamed for causing deviant behavior.

EARLY RESEARCH ON CHICANOS BY CHICANOS

In keeping with the treatment of the community as independent variable and "blaming the victim" perspectives, some researchers have linked low academic achievement by Mexican Americans to the population's cultural characteristics. Studies by Audrey Schwartz and C. Wayne Gorson were critically reviewed in Deluvina Hernandez's monograph *Mexican-American Challenge to a Sacred Cow* (1970). Hernandez's work is probably the first published academic piece written by a Chicana.

Social scientists assert that the Mexican American seeks immediate gratification through manipulative, expressive behavior and through emphasis on "scheming." Their study establishes Chicanos as deviant and abnormal or ineffective in their behavior. It supports racist stereotypes that Chicanos are untrustworthy and dishonest. This is also a stereotype that is upheld in movies (Keller 1985).

Schwartz and Gorson, among others, concluded that the root of low achievement by Mexican American youths is transmitted by one generation to another and is founded in Chicano culture, which is transmitted orally by the family. The implication is that what is being taught by the family—culture—is dysfunctional, and that only in breaking away from the family, its values, and its teachings will Chicanos gain upward mobility by succeeding in education.

These false conclusions established the Chicano as primary candidate for the "culture of poverty" perspective (a blame-the-victim perspective), which places severe blame on the family. This approach maintains that Chicano problems can be solved by dissociating from family influence and Chicano culture, which inhibit achievement. This analysis does not acknowledge structural forces that prevent Chicanos from attaining higher levels of performance.

There are many myths surrounding the study of Chicanos, especially Chicano families (Griswold del Castillo 1984). The above two studies exemplify what was found to be consistent treatment of Mexican Americans by non-Chicano social scientists earlier in this century. Chicano social scientists have strongly criticized much of this work. The first well-known criticism came from Octavio Romano in "The Anthropology and Sociology of the Mexican Americans" (1968b). Other highly critical works include studies by Florence Kluckhohn and Fred Strodbeck (1961), Celia Heller (1966), William Madsen (1964), and Richard Lamanna and the Chicano sociologist Julian Samora (1967).

At the time of early Chicano scholarship, Mexican Americans could not understand why Julian Samora, an advocate of Chicano civil rights, would engage in such repressive scholarship. The participation of Samora and of others like him in oppressive social science can be understood. It had little to do with Samora, the person and his beliefs. The structure of social science models was inherently demeaning and discriminatory to racial and ethnic minorities.

This means that the theoretical models, their assumptions, their interpretations, and their conclusions were incorrect or have/had something wrong with them. The problem is/was with the paradigms under which early scholars had to work. Some of these paradigms are still used today. They were culturally biased. Paradigms are the largest, most dominant, bodies of knowledge or theoretical perspectives in a science. In the social sciences they contain basic assumptions about the structure and function of society and its individuals. It is these assumptions, and how they are used to analyze the Chicano, that have frequently harmed the population.

Early Chicano scholars had to respond to a large body of literature that consistently contended that Chicanos had failed to organize politically. Failure to organize was deemed to be at the heart of their social problems. Lack of political organization had prevented upward mobility, assimilation, acculturation, and accommodation. These traits were considered valuable by established social scientists. Chicano scholars noted that society did not invite Chicano assimilation and accommodation—that, in fact, it erected barriers. One of the barriers was how social scientists defined various aspects of reality.

The Chicano scholar Raymond A. Rocco (1976) accurately contended that, unlike what Anglo social scientists believed, Chicanos have had a long history of organization. He included in his discussion a long list of Mexican American organizations in the Southwest:

Alianza Hispanomericana

Mexican Congress

Liga Protectora Mexicana

Orden Mejor de América

Community Service Organization

League of United Latin American Citizens

American G. I. Forum

Mexican American Political Association

Council of Mexican American Affairs

Political Association of Spanish-Speaking Organizations

Congress of Mexican American Unity

To this list can be added many, many more organizations, including some very early ones:

La Confederación de Uniones Obreras Mexicanas

Los Hermanos Penitentes

Las Gorras Blancas

American Democratic Organization

United Farm Workers

Crusade for Justice

El Partido de La Raza Unida

La Alianza Federal de Mercedes

Coalition on Human Rights and Immigration Policy

National Council of La Raza

National Association of Chicano Studies
National Association of Bilingual Education

Early in the study of Chicanos, it was discovered that traditional social scientists have too narrow a conception of what constitutes organization. They do not recognize that, like black organizations (DuBois 1967), many Mexican American organizations serve several purposes other than that of political organization. They fulfill a multiplicity of social, religious, economic, and educational functions at the same time. These are highly sophisticated, multifaceted organizations that approach their communities in a holistic manner and are different from the more narrowly defined organizational structure of Anglo Americans. This "lack of political organization" perspective also does not analyze the social system for structural discriminatory tendencies.

UPDATING THE SOCIAL SCIENCES

Traditional academic study of the Chicano also has not analyzed the population within a social historical context. It does not acknowledge that American society has problems with Chicanos. If Chicanos have problems, it is because the structure of that society causes most their problems. Even when the concept of assimilation is extended, dominant social scientists pose the dominant culture as the one into which Chicanos should assimilate. Social science does not experiment with the idea that the dominant culture might want to assimilate into Chicano culture or to negotiate a compromise.

Social scientists also have neglected the barrio as a viable community. They have ignored income and class variances within it and have neglected the fact that these variances produce differences in beliefs, values, and folkways. In an attempt to simplify Mexican life by suggesting that Mexicans are all alike, they feed racist-sexist discriminatory tendencies.

Race relations theory has focused upon dominant-subordinate power relations, but not upon the coping mechanisms created by racial and ethnic minorities. The focus on power also has steered social scientists away from a discussion of a form of American caste, a highly rigid system of stratification in which people's position is ascribed and in which there is minimal mobility.

This highly rigid system of social stratification prescribes for ethnic-racial minorities and women the roles they are to live down to. It ascribes low status and low social worth to individuals on the basis of color, culture, and history. This degradation is rationalized as the basis for unequal distribution of resources. Resources in the American capitalistic system are important. People of color with limited resources are constantly further degraded, devalued, and discriminated against. It is a vicious cycle. In addition, when social scientists' focus has been on color, it has been on black people, primarily on the east coast. This neglects and inadvertently denies the existence of discrimination in the West and throughout the entire country.

There are other severe faults and inaccuracies in traditional inattention to Mexican Americans. One of the most important is in the area of the family. Most social scientists romanticize the poor Mexican family. They view it as poor but cohesive and supportive, with an occasional violent outburst. This takes away from the reality of the hardships that people endure and totally neglects racist/sexist stereotypes.

Romanticization also takes attention away from the role of the social structure in creating poverty and misery. The overromanticization and attention to family outbursts diminish the violence and frustration of dominant-minority relations and, once again, imply dysfunctional families. Most Americans do not recognize discrimination as institutionalized frustration and violence. Most traditional scholars have given no attention to the coping and maintenance elements of the Chicano family.

Social scientists are continually challenged to defend their research methodologies and theoretical models. It is, therefore, incumbent upon students and scholars to attend academic conferences where these ideas are exchanged. Fallacies and misconceptions must not be allowed to continue unchallenged, especially in publications, for they contaminate the social sciences. Misleading social science perspectives do the society a great deal of harm, and they also harm the quality of science. They set the standard. These studies negatively impact and haunt racial/ethnic people for a long time. They also harm nonminority citizens. Nonminorities receive inaccurate information and cannot grow to be informed social participants.

For example, most Americans have assumed that assimilation is good, that integration of minority groups is correct and desirable. They have proceeded with this assumption because they are socialized to believe in democracy, and that in a democracy the majority rules.

Thus, Americans assume Chicanos, for example, should change to be like the dominant members of society. When this happens, discrimination is legitimized, with little attention to the fact that assimilation puts an end to the minority group's existence as a distinct cultural group with its own direction. This is cultural genocide.

To the rational mind, support for the assumption that the majority rules is no longer appropriate. The reality is that power rules, not numbers. Minorities are large in numbers and low in power. In actuality the minority, those fewer in number, rule in America. This is why the Chicano population, which is large in number, is the minority: it has relatively less power.

THE FUNCTION OF SOCIOLOGICAL THEORY

It has been noted that the study of the Chicano has been influenced by reigning theories in the social sciences. The two guiding schools of thought in sociology are the structural functional model and the conflict model.

For the study of Chicanos, these theoretical perspectives have shortcomings. The diversity of minority groups cannot be understood through utilization of theories grounded in experiences outside Chicano or other minority groups. Theories about specific groups must be based on that group's experience. The conflict model, however, has contributed significantly to the building of a Chicano perspective.

Another theory, the assimilation or melting pot theory, assumes that minority assimilation is desired and will be evidenced by intermarriage and the sharing of customs, attitudes, and skills. Assimilation may be rapid, as was that of European immigrants, or it may be much slower, as has been the case with blacks. Examples are given of European immigrants who have experienced disadvantaged social conditions but, through hard work and the adoption of dominant ways, have experienced social gains. It is posited that if Chicanos follow the example of the European immigrants, they will experience social gains.

Since much of the social science literature on Mexican Americans prior to 1970 was based upon an assimilation model of race relations, a review of the model is warranted. Basically, the model is this: America is the land of the free and the land of opportunity. In society there are mechanisms or social institutions, such as education, by which Chicanos can become part of the dominant system. They can take advantage of these mechanisms by becoming part of the system and by working hard. If Chicanos, or any population, have not experienced success, it is because they are not working hard enough.

Chicanos have not become part of the system despite their hard work. Most Americans blame the Chicanos themselves for not having experienced upward mobility. (For an excellent discussion on "blaming the victim," see William Ryan's *Blaming the Victim* [1976].) Basically, Ryan maintains that the educational system has inherent discriminatory tendencies that cause blacks to look as if they are failing in America's schools. This approach may be extended to include most racial and ethnic minorities.

The institution of education—what it is, how it exists, and what it does—fails minorities and pushes them out of school. Social discrimination manifests itself in such a way that at many levels of it, minorities appear to be failing when actually that is not what is happening at all. When extending the "blaming the victim" perspective to Chicanos, one discovers that they have formulated many creative techniques for coping with institutionalized racism. Dropping out of school is one of them. These techniques will be further examined in another chapter.

Implied in the melting pot theory is change, radical change. Giving up an ethnic culture is painful. Assimilation also has hurt those who have retained their culture. The system is rather intolerant of resistance to assimilation. Many northern and southern Europeans continue to suffer discrimination even though they have assimilated. Chicanos have not melted. They have not assimilated. They have been intermarrying, sharing cultures, attitudes, and various skills with the dominant society, for over 200 years.

For a more accurate analysis one must accept the fact that Native Americans, Chicanos, and blacks did not come to the United States voluntarily. They also did not immigrate. The Chicanos were conquered in an imperialistic war. Blacks were forcibly brought in as slaves. Native Americans, who were here before the Anglos, also were conquered, placed on reservations, and severely punished if they left. The United States wanted more territory, more railroads, more minerals, and more cheap labor. It purposefully set out to start the Mexican American War in order to acquire what it wanted: Mexico's northern territories (Acuna 1981).

The condition of introduction into the United States is important.

Those who did not enter voluntarily were subjected to even more severe discrimination than their voluntary-immigrant European counterparts. Voluntary immigrants knew that if they came to America, they would have to change. Apartheid, conquest, slavery, and force do not set up conditions for cultural abnegation. People of color were/are not invited into the white system. These people are too culturally different and, above all, they are not white.

Social scientists are questioning the use of the melting pot theory to explain and predict the conditions of ethnic and racial minorities in the United States. Some have stopped using it altogether. It is wishful thinking and oppressive social science to employ perspectives rooted in an immigrant experience that does not apply to Chicanos. Hispanics and Native Americans were in what is now the United States long before the white men came. They had settled, learned to live, and developed societies in the Southwest long before the White settlers arrived. The Spanish were the first white people to settle on this continent. They had thriving villages and cities such as Santa Fe, New Mexico, the oldest capital city in the United States. However, the average American student does not learn this in school. Education and the retention of knowledge have become political tools used in discrimination.

Discrimination, although it has drastically hurt some of the population, nevertheless has been extremely helpful. It limits competition for what are considered scarce resources: money, power, status, and prestige. These resources are not scarce. They are concentrated among a few people. The American public has been led to believe that education is the way one achieves these resources, but discrimination in education keeps competitors in reserve and does not fully allow people of color to compete for resources.

ACCEPTING THE MIRANDE CHALLENGE

In 1985, the Chicano sociologist Alfredo Mirande called for a Chicano sociology that developed and accepted a new perspective. This perspective was to be part of a broader movement to develop nontraditional paradigms. In the *Chicano Experience* he outlines the social science models formulated on the basis of European groups who immigrated voluntarily. He asserts, correctly, that this model does not apply to Chicanos. Like other Chicano social scientists, he declares that the Mexican experience was initially one of conquest and not of immigration. The population exists as a conquered population, internally colonized and excluded from formal participation in American society. In essence there are unwritten rules that apply to Chicanos that do not apply uniformly to all Americans. Mirande also accurately contends that Chicano culture is still being presented as disorganized and pathological.

After many years of producing a Chicano perspective, Chicano social scientists are still placed in the position of correcting what is not true. This places Chicano scholars in a reactionary position and frequently does not allow the development of more creative thinking. It also keeps them from fully accepting the Mirande challenge; but it does keep them within the realm of the dialogue. This fact in itself is very important, for it was not until roughly the mid–1970s that Chicanos were allowed to participate in the dialogue. The reader should keep in mind that Chicanos had to assert their right to participate.

The Mirande challenge can be accepted by the social sciences. The issue of disorganized and pathological culture is mute. Chicano culture is an integrative force that is organized and successfully guides its members. Research needs to be conducted on how this culture is organized. It is asserted that it is not conceptualized in a linear fashion but more in a holistic manner that is circular. If pathology exists in Chicano culture, it exists because the social system imposes conditions that produce it. This does not negate that populations will produce their own kind of pathology. However, at this time scholars cannot assess pathology because they do not have an operational definition of it and because of unidentified intervening variables that are associated with dominant social forces.

Chicano culture should be analyzed as a force possessing mechanisms that enable individuals to cope with the oppression of discrimination. This requires positive, crative energy, energy that limits Chicano competition. Scholars who depict Chicano culture as disorganized and pathological have not kept up with contemporary social science and have forgotten what they should have learned in introductory sociology: Racism is functional; culture is shared knowledge, and it is relative. What people know and how they do things are normal for their culture and their circumstances. What is normal for one group is not always normal for another. It is the pathological social scientists who do not recognize that their way of thinking is correct only for them and their culture.

Meeting the Mirande challenge means involving oneself in a holistic critical analysis. For example, Mirande notes that most sociological research instruments are validated on members of the majority (white) society and are then imposed on Chicanos. The truth is that Chicanos are not white and have not received white social treatment and privileges. Thus, not all sociological findings address Chicano social reality. Some Chicano social scientists have duplicated the established academic mechanisms and have found it difficult to escape their Anglo-favoring web. This happens because Chicano social scientists are trained in white institutions by, primarily, white male professors. In order to survive in white-male-dominated institutions, they frequently internalize teachings without fully knowing that the teachings are inherently racist and sexist, and in many ways oppressive to some populations.

Future instruction and research must focus on how this takes place. It is suggested that this be addressed in discussions about value neutrality and objectivity. Mirande notes that value neutrality and objectivity have been used against scholars who do minority research and theory construct as a means to keep them within the confines of oppressive social science. This, of course, affects the social sciences by maintaining the status quo and not advancing knowledge.

THE ROLE OF DISCRIMINATION

There is another challenge that invites attention. This involves the discussion and elimination of discrimination. In order to understand the social role of discrimination, we must first understand the nature of the dominant American culture. It is individualistic, upwardly mobile, competitive, and profit oriented, and puts a high value on progress. At the same time that these characteristics have shaped one of the strongest countries in the world, they have harmed many Americans.

Most Americans are too busy living their lives to think about defining and questioning their cultural values. These cultural values have produced an ideology that strongly appreciates success. Success in America usually means obtaining large amounts of many resources, especially money. In Chicano culture success means stability, growing old, and living in peace. Money and resources are also valued; but in contrast with most Americans, Chicanos do not live their lives continuously seeking progress and with profit in mind.

For dominant America the preoccupation with profit usually is translated into doing what will acquire more: more money, more clothes, more private property, more time, more of everything.

Progress is akin to wanting more; it means changing things, making them better, quicker, faster. In order to keep up the turbulent pace, Americans must be competitive. This means being better than everyone else and surpassing everyone who wants the same thing. Chicano culture teaches communal values. People are members of the same human community and are not to be competed against. In fact, the culture teaches that community members assist one another.

Some discrimination is institutional, part of the social fabric. Some of it is more direct. In either case, discrimination limits competition and gives social advantage to nonminorities. Through discrimination people are kept poor, uneducated, and oppressed to the point where they frequently blame themselves for not succeeding.

Future chapters will focus more on cultural differences and similarities, and how discrimination functions. Perhaps the model most applicable to the Chicano experience is the internal colonial model, but it needs a more sociological and a feminist perspective.

THE INTERNAL COLONIAL MODEL

Sexism has its basis in sexual characteristics and, like racism, its basis is biologically inappropriate. Persons possessing certain chracteristics play male or female roles according to how those characteristics are defined. Males have had a history of being attributed more social value, and often male superiority has crawled into the social sciences. Feminists are very critical of such perspectives. They have claimed sexism because the disciplines have not documented the female experience and have not allowed women to contribute to the acquisition of knowledge. In the case of Chicanos and Chicanas, social science has been both sexist and racist (Mirande and Enríquez 1979). The contributions and the role of Spanish-speaking people have not been documented or presented. Most severely lacking is the role of the Mexican American female, the Chicana.

Chicano social scientists have analyzed Chicano subjects by use of the internal colonial model. The exclusion of Chicanas is apparent. The model is based upon the work of Robert Blauner, who drew upon the work of Frantz Fanon and Albert Memmi, both of whom wrote extensively about colonization. According to Fanon (1963), colonization is a process based upon violence. Violence is used by the colonizers against the colonized to gain cheap labor, land, and other resources, and to retain them. Violence is turned inward by the colonized because of frustration and suppressed aggression felt toward the colonizers, whom they aspire to be like. Further, violence is directed toward the colonizers, who are finally seen as the real enemy. The process is terminated only through ultimate violence: revolution by the colonized. In summary, colonization is the process by which the lives and land of indigenous people of color are secured and maintained by a foreign group through power and violence.

Memmi (1965) advances the view that segregation and discrimination are part of the colonial system. The colonizers force the colonized to live separately in conditions inferior to those of the colonizers, who possess special privileges based on economic position and color. Even the poorest colonizers have privileges over the colonized and believe they are superior. In addition, the colonizers advance stereotypes about the colonized and their inferior status, thereby reinforcing discrimination and prejudice against the colonized. The colonized, unable to get out of the situation, internalize the stereotypes and as a result have low attainment and low self-esteem. Low attainment strengthens the stereotype and furthers discrimination and prejudice against the colonized.

Memmi continues by noting that the colonizers will use those members of the colonized who most resemble them by moving them to the periphery of both groups through encouraging selected colonized individuals to work for the colonizers by acting as "go-betweens." This technique robs the colonized group of leadership and ensures that they will be kept in a subservient social position. Many times the colonized will reject their origin and identify themselves, as much as possible, with the colonizers. According to Memmi, the colonizers will never fully accept the "go-betweens" because they believe colonized persons are of an inferior race with an inferior culture.

Robert Blauner (1972) applies the colonial model primarily to the American black population but writes that it also serves to explain the Chicano experience. In relationship to the Chicano condition there is a problem with the model: unlike black Americans, the population has not been subject to unfree labor. It must be mentioned, however, that many Americans speculated that Mexicans were seen by some white advocates of the Mexican American War as being the next population to be enslaved.

Black Americans, unlike Chicanos, have a history of living close to white people on white property and in their homes. Blauner writes that colonized populations have historically been rural. Although the Chicanos are overwhelmingly urban today, the population has its historical roots in rural, mountain, and urban settings. Finally, Blauner writes that colonized populations have a history of not being able to organize. Unlike traditional colonized populations, the Chicano population has an unrecognized history of organization.

Rodolfo Acuna (1972) contends that the parallels between the Chicano experience in the United States and the colonization of other people are too similar to dismiss. The conquest of the Southwest created a colonial situation in the traditional sense, with Mexican land and population being controlled by an imperialistic United States. It is Acuna's and other Chicano scholars' further contention that the situation exists today in the form of an internal colony. Even though Acuna became critical of the model in his second edition of *Occupied America,* Chicano scholars draw the following parallels between the Chicanos' experience and the colonization of other Third World peoples.

- Indigenous people had their land invaded by people from another country. The colonizer later used additional military force to gain and maintain control.
- The original inhabitants involuntarily became subjects of the conquerors.
- The conquered had an alien culture and government imposed upon them.
- The conquered became victims of racism and cultural genocide, and were relegated to a submerged status.
- The conquered were rendered politically and economically powerless.
- The conquerors felt they had a "mission" in occupying the area in question and believed they had undeniable privileges by virtue of their conquest.

Acuna agrees with Blauner that there is a distinct difference that impedes universal acceptance of the reality of Anglo colonialism. The land taken from Mexico bordered the United States rather than being an area geographically distant from the "mother country." Acuna accuses American historians of having subconsciously accepted the myth that the area was always intended to be an integral part of the United States. Instead of conceptualizing the conquered territory as northern Mexico, they perceive it in terms of the "American Southwest."

Acuna also accuses American historians of believing that the Southwest was won in fair and just warfare, as opposed to unjust imperialism. He writes that in the case of Texas, historians believe Mexico attacked the peace-loving Anglos. Ethnocentric American historians believe that imperialism is an affliction of other countries and not of their own. They do so in spite of the fact that a study of American history as it developed from east to west clearly illustrates imperialist tactics.

The issue of imperialism, however, never surfaces because it is not called imperialism. Chicano studies, which considers history from south to north, emphasizes the imperialist nature of the United States. This approach has made Chicano studies unpopular with some dominant white historians and citizens who have internalized the "peace-loving" myth in American history.

Other historians and social scientists maintain that colonization continues, but that it is now occurring within the country rather than being imposed by an external power. These social scientists extend the internal colonial model. The relationship between Anglos and Chicanos remains the same, that of master and servant. The principal difference is that after hundreds of years, Mexicans in the traditional colonies are nearly indigenous to the conquered land. While some are descendants of people who lived in the area long before the end of the war with Mexico, large numbers are technically descendants of more recent immigrants. The internal colonial model incorporates these immigrants into its perspective because they inherit traditional dominant-subordinate relations.

A REVIEW OF CHICANO SOCIAL HISTORY

After 1910 almost one-eighth of Mexico's population immigrated to the United States. The original colonies expanded in size with this increased immigration and new settlements sprang up. These settlements added to the nation-within-a-nation. Psychologically, socially, and culturally they remained Mexican and Spanish-speaking, but had little or no control of the dominant political, economic, or educational structures that affected them.

These structures critically affected the quality of life both within and outside the barrio. Anglos controlled the barrios or *colonias*. They designed educational curricula that did not meet the needs of Chicano students but instead served to "Americanize" them. In addition, police patrolling the *colonia* lived, for the most part, outside the area. Acuna contends that their purpose was to protect Anglo property against Mexican intrusion.

Anglos owned the business and industry located in the *colonia*. Thus, all profit was taken out of the barrio. This pattern is one that emerged in most Chicano communities and continues to exist today. Barrio residents referred to themselves as living in the *colonia*. They linguistically and politically acknowledged their social circumstance.

Mario Barrera (1979) and Carlos Muñoz (1972) view the characteristic distinguishing between internal and external colonialism as the legal status of the colonized. According to their interpretation, a colony can be considered internal if the colonized population has the same formal legal status as any other group of citizens, and external if it is placed in a separate legal category. It is external if it is even partly excluded from equal participation. Chicano communities in the United States are internal colonies, for they occupy a status of formal equality regardless of what the informal reality may be.

The development of the Southwest and the influence of colonialism have affected the Chicano at the social, political, and economic levels. At the economic level the influence is based on a division of labor whereby Chicanos supply cheap labor. Former Chicano land provides the resources necessary for production. At the same time the Chicanos provide a consumer market.

The internal colonial model is a social-historical model. It notes that the vast discrepancy in economic and political power levels did not always exist between the Chicanos and the Anglos. In fact, it was not until the early 1800s that the two entered into any kind of relationship.

The Chicanos' Indian ancestors, however, felt a colonial influence in the 1500s when the Spanish conquest brought colonialism to Mexico. By 1521 the *encomienda* (estate granted by Spanish kings) system was established and Spanish landowners had gained control of the Indians, who up to that time had controlled their people and land without any interference from the white man. The *encomienda* gave Spanish landowners a certain number of Indians, who were forced to work on the farms and in the mines. Work was supposedly done in exchange for instruction in the Roman Catholic faith. Great estates were established by displacing the Indians from the land and the villages.

The power of the Catholic Church has always been felt in Mexico and in the American Southwest. The first Spanish missionaries, the Franciscans, arrived in Mexico in 1524, and by 1553 the first institution of higher education in North America was founded in Mexico City. Colonialism gained a firmer hold, and by 1557 silver was mined and exported to Spain. In 1720 the *encomienda* system was officially abolished, but the exploitation of the Indians continued.

There arose three distinct social categories: the *indios,* who outnumbered all others, were the lowest class. The mestizos, of mixed Indian and Spanish blood, and the privileged pure Spanish were split into two other classes, the colonial-born Creoles and the Spanish-born *gachupines.* The populltion also included a group of black people who eventually merged with the mestizos. Instrumental in formulating these social relationships was the church, which by the late 1700s had acquired great wealth and political power.

A significant year for Chicano people and for Mexico was 1810. That year Miguel Hidalgo, a Creole priest, called for independence from Spain and from the exploitation of its colonialism. To protect and call for liberation from exploitation, and in recognition of Father Hidalgo's famous "grito de Dolores," Chicanos hold fiestas and political rallies on September 16. Non-Chicanos often confuse September 16 festivities with the Cinco de Mayo. Both of these days are independence commemorations, much like the Fourth of July. On May 5, Mexican independence from the French is celebrated. This celebration is not to be confused with the Mexican American War, which does not call for Chicano celebration.

In 1835–1836, conflict grew between Mexican officials and Anglo farmers who had been given land grants in what is now Texas. A complex series of events, including the abolition of slavery by Mexico on September 9, 1829, led to open revolt by American citizens in 1835 and to a declaration of Texas' independence from Mexico on March 2, 1836 (Acuna 1972). Throughout this time Texans continued to defy Mexican laws. Mexico viewed Texans as undermining the authority of their host, which had allowed them to settle in the area at no cost. Texans wanted Texas to be part of the United States and not under Mexican authority.

The annexation of Texas by the United States in December 1845 was the main cause of the Mexican-American War. The Mexican government refused to enter into diplomatic talks concerning the sale of California and New Mexico, both of which were claimed by Texas. American capitalists who sought to extend the slave-holding territories of the United States called for war. Disagreements over territorial boundaries brought gunfire near Brownsville, Texas; and on May 13, 1846, after much preparation, the American Congress declared war on ill-prepared Mexico. Fighting was already taking place, and war quickly spread as far as New Mexico and Veracruz.

The Treaty of Guadalupe Hidalgo brought the Mexican-American War to an end on February 2, 1848. Mexico lost the war primarily because it was torn by internal political strife and because it had no idea that the United States would resort to war. The victory brought the United States two-fifths of Mexican territory: California, Arizona, New Mexico, Utah, Nevada, and part of Colorado, and agreement to the 1845 annexation of Texas.

The Treaty of Guadalupe Hidalgo offered full American citizenship to Mexican citizens who lived north of the Rio Grande border. Residents had one year to choose Mexican or American citizenship. Many chose to stay on the land that had been theirs for generations, where they shared similar lives with other northern Mexicans. The Treaty of Guadalupe Hidalgo also guaranteed civil liberties, property rights, cultural rights, and linguistic and religious freedom. The treaty was broken, however, and former Mexican citizens were victimized by Texas Rangers and other vigilante groups who killed, kidnapped, and harassed Chicanos.

The racist Anglos did everything in their power to dehumanize the Chicano people. They acted in a true imperialist, colonial fashion in an attempt to get the Chicanos to internalize racist-sexist messages that they were inferior and Anglos were superior. The Mexican culture was vulgarized and Mexican heroes were made to look like rebels, murderers, and bandits. Mexican women were stereotyped as prostitutes, passive, disease-infected, loose, and victims of Chicano male brutality.

SUMMARY

The contemporary Chicano still seeks to overcome racist-sexist stereotypes advanced by Anglos and sometimes internalized by Chicanos. Chicano studies classes at universities and colleges struggle to overcome biased curricula. Chicanas have struggled not only at an intellectual level but also at a community level, where theories are being discussed and attempts at putting such theories into practice are being made.

The Chicana, however, is in an unusual situation. She cannot separate being female from being brown. She struggles to address sexism in her own culture as well as in the general society, and she also seeks to overcome the historical conditions of poverty and exploitation of her people.

For struggling against these factors, the Chicano people have been attacked verbally, physically, and psychologically. On one hand the Chicanos are called un-American and radical for being critical and resisting. On the other hand, the population continues to be physically, socially, and culturally beaten. Such violence has taken place on picket lines and at demonstration rallies, in prison and in private settings. The violence seeps into Chicano homes, schools, and churches. Policies that discriminate continue to be both legal and illegal. These laws, both written and unwritten, have served to keep Chicanos "in their place": a place of low economic and political power, low health, and low education.

REFERENCES

Acuna, Rodolf. 1972. *Occupied America: Struggle Toward Chicano Liberation.* San Francisco: Canfield.

——, 1981. *Occupied America: A History of Chicanos.* 2nd ed. of *Occupied America* (1972). New York: Harper and Row.

Baca-Zinn, Maxine. 1975. "Political Familism: Toward Sex Role Equality in Chicano Families." *Aztlan: Chicano Journal of the Social Sciences and the Arts* (Spring): 13–26.

Barrera, Mario. 1979. *Race and Class in the Southwest: A Theory of Racial Inequality.* South Bend, IN: University of Notre Dame Press.

Blauner, Robert. 1972. *Racial Oppression in America.* New York: Harper and Row.

Blea, Irene I. 1980. "Bessemer: A Sociological Perspective of a Chicano Barrio." Ph.D. diss., University of Colorado, Boulder.

——. 1988. *Bessemer: A Sociological Perspective of a Chicano Barrio.* New York: AMS Press.

Coser, Lexis A. 1959. *The Functions of Social Conflict.* Glencoe, IL: Free Press.

Dahrendorf, Ralf. 1959. *Class and Class Conflict in Industrial Society.* Palo Alto, CA: Stanford University Press.

Davis, Allison. 1941. *Deep South.* South Bend, IN: University of Notre Dame Press.

Dollard, John, 1937. *Caste and Class in a Southern Town.* New Haven: Yale University Press.

Drake, Sinclair, and Horace Cayton. 1945. *Black Metropolis.* New York: Harcourt, Brace and World.

DuBois, W. E. B. 1967. *The Philadelphia Negro.* New York: Benjamin Blam.

Fanon, Frantz. 1963. *The Wretched of the Earth.* New York: Grove Press.

Gans, Herbert J. 1962. *The Urban Villagers.* New York: Free Press.

Glazer, Nathan and Daniel Moynihan. 1963. *Beyond the Melting Pot: The Negros, Puerto Ricans, Jews, Italians and Irish of New York City.* Cambridge, MA: MIT Press.

Griswold del Castillo, Richard. 1984. *La Familia: Chicano Families in the Urban Southwest, 1848 to the Present.* South Bend, IN: University of Notre Dame Press.

Heller, Celia. 1966. *Mexican American Youth: Forgotten Youth at the Crossroads.* New York: Random House.

Hernández, Deluvina. 1970. *Mexican-American Challenge to a Sacred Cow.* Los Angeles: Chicano Cultural Center.

Hollingshead, August B. 1949. *Elmtown's Youth.* New York: John Wiley and Sons.

Keller, Gary D. 1985. *Chicano Cinema: Research, Reviews, and Resources.* Binghamton, NY: Bilingual Review Press.

Kluckhohn, Florence, and Fred L. Strodbeck. 1961. *Variation in Value Orientations.* Evanston, IL: Race Peterson.

Lamanna, Richard A., and Julian Samora. 1967. *Mexican Americans in a Midwest Metropolis.* Los Angeles: Mexican American Project.

Leibow, Elliot. 1967. *Tally's Corner: A Study of Negro Streetcorner Men.* Boston: Little, Brown.

Lewis, Oscar. 1959. *Five Families.,* New York: New American Library.

Lynd, Robert S. and Helen M. Lynd. 1929. *Middletown: A Study of Contemporary American Culture.* New York: Harcourt, Brace.

Madsen, William. 1964. *Mexican Americans of South Texas.* New York: Holt, Rinehart and Winston.

Marx, Karl. 1955. *Communist Manifesto.* Chicago: Henry Regnery.

Memmi, Albert. 1965. *The Colonizer and the Colonized.* Boston: Beacon Press.

Mirande, Alfredo. 1985. *The Chicano Experience.* South Bend, IN: University of Notre Dame Press.

Mirande, Alfredo, and Evangelina Enríquez. 1979. *La Chicana.* Chicago: University of Chicago Press.

Montiel, Miguel. 1970. "The Social Science Myth of the Mexican American Family." *El Grito: A Journal of Contemporary Mexican American Thought"* (Summer): 56–63.

Moore, Joan W., Robert García, Carlos García, Luis Cerda, and Frank Valencia. 1979. *Homeboys: Gangs, Drugs and Prison in the Barrios of Los Angeles.* Philadelphia: Temple University Press.

Muñoz, Carlos, Jr. 1972. "The Politics of Urban Protest: A Model of Political Analysis." Ph.D. diss., Claremont College, Graduate School of Government.

Murguia, Edward. 1975. *Assimilation, Colonialism and the Mexican American People.* Los Angeles: Mexican American Monograph Series, no. 1.

Nisbet, Robert A. 1962. *Community and Power: A Study in the Ethics of Order and Freedom.* New York: Oxford University Press.

Parsons, Talcott. 1954. *Essays on Sociological Theory.* Glencoe, IL: Free Press.

Poplin, Dennis E. 1972. *Communities: A Survey of Theories and Methods of Research.* New York: Macmillan.

Rocco, Raymond A. 1976. "The Chicano in the Social Sciences: Traditional Concepts, Myths and Images." *Aztlan: International Journal of Chicano Studies* (Spring).

Romano, Octavio V. 1968a. "Editorial." *El Grito: A Journal of Contemporary Mexican American Thought* 2 (Fall): 2–4.

———. 1968b. "The Anthropology and Sociology of the Mexican Americans: The Distortion of Mexican-American History." *El Grito: A Journal of Contemporary Mexican American Thought* 2 (Fall): 13–16.

Ryan, William. 1976. *Blaming the Victim.* New York: Vintage Books.

Saunders, Lyle. 1954. *Cultural Differences and Medical Care of the Spanish-Speaking People in the Southwest.* New York: Russell Sage Foundation.

Schulz, David A. 1969. *Coming up Black: Patterns of Ghetto Socialization.* Englewood Cliffs, NJ: Prentice-Hall.

Tuck, Ruth. 1946. *Not with the Fist: Mexican Americans in a Southwest City.* New York: Harcourt, Brace.

Valentine, Charles. 1968. *Culture of Poverty: A Critique and Counter-proposal.* Chicago: University of Chicago Press.

Vidich, Arthur, and Joseph Bensman. 1958. *Small Town in Mass Society.* Princeton: Princeton University Press.

Warner, W. Lloyd, and Paul S. Lunt. 1941. *The Social Life of Modern Community.* New Haven: Yale University Press.

West, James. 1945. *Plainville, U.S.A.* New York: Columbia University Press.

Wirth, Louis. 1928. *The Ghetto.* Chicago: University of Chicago Press.

Whyte, William Foote. 1955. *Street Corner Society.* Chicago: University of Chicago Press.

2
Social Stratification by Race, Class, and Gender

INTRODUCTION

Americans live in a hierarchically stratified society. Social stratification is an institutionalized system by which people are placed into layered categories, then negatively or positively ranked according to social worth. Social stratification is characterized by unequal distribution of resources that produce wealth for some. Wealth, power, and prestige emerge as linked social variables; and if one is high in wealth, power and prestige usually (but not always) follow.

Wealth usually is equal to money and how many resources one controls, and manifests itself in power. Prestige is more subjective and is dependent on how one is perceived and valued by others. It is much like status, which is social honor measured by how much a person is revered. Social status draws those who are socially alike and is linked to social honor. In an attempt to simplify the social impact of the above variables, social scientists often collapse them into "socioeconomic status," which is the composite measure of a person's social worth and place in society. Socioeconomic status is also granted according to race, class, and gender.

THE IMPACT OF SOCIAL STRATIFICATION

Research on the impact of social stratification on Chicanos incorporates European perspectives such as those of Max Weber (Gerth and Mills 1946) and Karl Marx (Engels 1967). Marx has been most popular because he differentiates between the poor and the rich, the workers and the nonworkers, the proletariat and the capitalists, the powerless and the powerful, and maintains that they compose two classes.

Marxist theory contends that in a capitalistic economy (such as that of the United States) social stratification and inequality are an inevitable outcome of private property, the division of labor, and exploitation of workers by capitalists. The capitalists control the means of production and distribution of goods: land and other resources (such as tools, factories, offices, and stores). Capitalists do not work. Workers do not control resources. They control only the labor power in their bodies and, because of this, are forced to work for the capitalists. The capitalist owners of the means of production have the objective of maximizing profit by minimizing wages.

This inevitable and unjust social arrangement does not benefit society; it benefits the capitalists. Marxists contend that poor workers will rebel against the capitalists. Workers will eventually gain class consciousness and come to a full realization of their miserable, alienated, exploited condition; then they will overthrow the capitalists.

The Marxist perspective has strongly impacted Chicano academics, as well as community ideology and political activity. This is not to be interpreted to mean that most Chicanos are Marxists. They are not.

Barrera (1979) and Muñoz (1972) went further than most Marxists by extending the impact of race and caste on class structure. Although their work is admirable, there is further need to incorporate an approach that addresses not only class struggle but also race and gender dimensions, as well as more complete discussion on the ideas of revolution, liberation, and decolonization.

Sociologists Alfredo Mirande (1985) and Tomas Almaguer (1975) agree that race transcends class, as does gender, which transcends class and exchanges position with race. This makes it difficult to fully appreciate the elements of social control on minority women (which also affects minority men).

A quick survey of America's stratified social system reveals that disproportionate numbers of people of color are poor and have low socioeconomic status. Among the lowest-ranked are black and Mexican American women with children. This feminization of poverty places women in a special category of people who have social chances stacked against them. The fact that poverty is overwhelmingly a woman-of-color characteristic suggests that it has its basis in the experience of being a female and a person of color at the same time. The United States is dominated by males who are white. Women of color endure more severe social discrimination than anyone else in the society.

The social structure bestows privilege upon white males. The majority of dominant white males value most the people who are like them. They want no competition because they do not want to share the social benefits and a life of relative comfort. They want other people to believe that these attributes and resources are rare and in short supply. This makes them more comfortable and valuable. To maintain the status quo (staying in socially preferred positions), the dominant exploit and divide the largest segment of society. Social class, racism, and sexism are created to keep people divided and unable to realize who is controlling and oppressing them. Token status, money, and privilege are given to those who play the most active divisive roles. Those who cannot, or will not, take part in this sytem are punished. Usually their punishment is poverty and lack of status, power, and prestige. If a group of like people feel or act outside their socially prescribed roles, the entire group is punished.

SOCIAL DEVIANCE THEORY AND STRATIFICATION

From the perspective of who is plotted where in the social system, perhaps a statistical deviation theory is the most effective. Social deviance models have more to do with who is considered abnormal in society. From a social deviance approach, the more a person deviates from the artificially constructed social norm (set up by those in control), the more social punishment he/she incurs. The persons most different from the established norms are racial-ethnic minorities and women. On a race-ethnic-gender scale, women of color rank the lowest. In other words, people possess ascribed value and worth because of who and what they are born. They have no control over this. Those who are too different from the artificially constructed norm are set up to be labeled and treated as social deviants.

Dominant members of society have not attached much social worth to white women, but white women are white and are valued more than people of color. Because white men control the economy, this becomes an important factor. Women of color find themselves consistently on the lowest rung of the socioeconomic ladder, but they sometimes appear to have more social mobility than do men of color.

The economic social institutions, such as the family, religion, and politics, channel human behavior and are consistent with the dominantly imposed norm. Women of color are grossly affected by the very foundation of what constitutes society. It is at this level of analysis that sociology and Chicano studies can make, and have made, their greatest contribution to the understanding of society and the social forces that support it.

SOCIAL STRATIFICATION AND THE IDEOLOGY OF LIBERATION

Chicanos in the 1960s recognized that their social position was characterized by poverty in the richest, most advanced country in the world. They forced the U.S. government to recognize that Chicanos were living in conditions characterized by lack of food, shelter, and health standards. In 1983, the number of Chicanos living under similar conditions rose to 15.2 percent. In 1984, there were approximately 35 million poor people in America. Chicanos were disproportionately represented among them (U.S. Bureau of the Census 1985). The Chicano capitalist experience has been characterized by hard labor, exploitation, and dual standards of worth asnd discrimination. Chicanos are disproportiontely represented in the poor and the working class, and this experience has given them a definite ideology.

From their relationships to the dominant structure, people emerge with an ideology. Ideology consists of a set of ideas about what fashions life: its norms and its values. It is a rationalization of the existing social structure, and it is idealistic. More often than not, there is a huge discrepancy bewteen what is real and what is ideal. In the United States the leading ideology is annexed to the American dream. The American dream is what most people believe about America and what they want from their country. Sociologists claim it rationalizes people's class position, functioning to make them accept it. Its assumption is that America is the land of the free, of justice for all, and of opportunity. The American dream alleges to all citizens, regardless of gender or color, that society is characterized by equality. All one has to do is work hard, and upward mobility will follow. If people do not work hard enough, they do not move up and out of their socioeconomic position.

An extension of this thought is that each person gets the class position he/she deserves. If blame or credit is to be given, the individual deserves it. Most people are not very critical of this perspective. They have no interest in changing their minds or of exposing the American dream as a myth or a fallacy. They want a piece of the best that America has to offer.

It is interesting to note that in this line of thinking, America and its role in society become illusive. It is as if America exists as a natural entity somewhere in the realm of the mystical. "America" and "the society" have become catchwords for very real things, but they are illusive catchwords when one considers that what is actually meant is the social system composed of, and linked to, social institutions that teach beliefs, values, and worths that manifest themselves as behaviors that work against certain kinds of people.

Added to this definition or understanding should be the latent and manifest structures and functions (subtle workings) of the system. These elements are more abstract, more theoretical mental constructs, and status quo social scientists resist criticizing them. They view a critical perspective as a value judgment. They resist because they do not like having their fundamental values questioned, exposed as not always right or honorable, or even as inherently discriminatory. Most human beings want to believe that they are righteous people. Rather than change their ideology and admit that perhaps they have been led into uncomfortable and even dishonorable beliefs and behaviors, they fight to maintain the status quo.

As stated before, the Chicano perspective is controversial. This makes Chicano studies both extremely popular and unpopular. It is popular with those who share its critical approach and seek liberation from controlling sources, and it is unpopular with those who adhere to the social psychological legitimization of a system that systemically oppresses people. It is often unpopular with Mexican Americans who refuse to engage in a critical sociological approach to how the society functions. They refuse to analyze who they are in a social-historical context, how they came to be citizens of this country, and the dominant-subordinate relationships established and maintained throughout history.

This resistant attitude has been constructed and related by the teaching of dominant American history and values in the schools. It is supported by the subtle, unchanging workings of what composes the camouflaged social fabric. In addition, Chicanos have internalized the American dream and live under a capitalist ideology, working hard in order to achieve the benefits they see accorded to the capitalists.

Lest we run the risk of stereotyping Mexican Americans, let us examine some of the factors that characterize them and their ideologies. Not all American Hispanics are poor or lack education. In fact, Hispanics are represented in the highest income brackets. Many have high status, power, and prestige. Many are doctors, attorneys, professors, political officials, architects, athletes, artists, scientists, engineers; and many have not only national but international reputations. Not all successful Hispanics have higher education but most do; and not all individuals with higher education are concentrated in high-status, higher-power, and high-prestige positions.

Research on how some Chicanos have escaped the traps of poverty and discrimination has yet to be conducted. The preliminary assumption is that some have escaped because they inherited the fruits of the hard work done by their parents and/or they forfeited much personal pleasure and utilized the limited vehicles of upward social mobility in very creative ways. These individuals dared to risk. Courageously and in isolation they crossed racial, class, and gender boundaries. They are, to varying degrees, bicultural; and they have endured personal failures, degradation, success, and marginality. Prejudice and discrimination do not hold everyone back and down, but only few escape.

Sociologist Peter Rose (1981) contends that the first reaction to oppression is submission. If minority group members accept inferior social status and prescribed social roles, they submit to the dominant group. The second reaction is withdrawal. People may accept inferior social position but may also withdraw from their own minority group. These people are generally ashamed of their group membership and attempt to succeed by passing as members of the dominant group. Withdrawal, like submission, may exact a high psychological price. Those who withdraw will, more than likely, not be totally accepted by the dominant group, or they may feel guilt and shame for having abandoned their people. They are what sociologists call marginal people, people who are caught between two cultural forces.

The third reaction to social oppression is separation. People who

separate recognize their inferior status, but they reject it. They segregate and live in barrios, ghettos, Chinatowns, or Polish, Italian,
or Irish neighborhoods where they establish their own support systems. This perspective assumes too much control by the ethnic community and negates existing outside social forces. A fourth reaction
to racism is integration. Integration rejects both inferior status and
segregation. This reaction strives to achieve equality within the dominant system. Integration, however, threatens ethnic identity and
generally leads to assimilation.

Rose neglected a fifth, more healthy reaction. Many people are
truly bicultural. They interact with their own people and with the
dominant group. Social scientists have yet to study this group, but
the following assumptions may apply. These people are highly sophisticated, with a sound understanding of the power and control of
the dominant system. They reject messages of minority inferiority,
and they do not accept segregation. They understand their people.
They see the value and the worth of their culture, and they desire
the benefits of capitalism. They accept that there are two systems.
They recognize the discrimination of the dominant system and the
victimization of their own people, as well as that of other people of
color and of women. These people often work to change the dominant system into a more humane society.

Bicultural Chicanos believe that there truly can be, and should be,
justice and equal opportunity. We can find members of this growing
group in every level of society. This reaction is a more healthy
reaction because there is no guilt, no shame, no self-deception, no
false expectations. The bicultural/bilingual reaction also gives the
individual a variety of social relationships, a more broadly defined
reality. It allows for more creativity and what should be a highly
valued social resource. This individual does not get caught in and
between two cultures, but moves well between both with a clear
ideology. There is only one drawback. These people may "burn
out." They work too hard to obtain equality, and experience tired-
ness and frustration. Thus, they must be careful to protect their
physical and mental health. It is believed that the "successful" Chicano is truly gifted and has a life-style patterned after the idea of
liberation or decolonization.

This calls into question the definition of success. Unlike the American normative definition of status, power, and money, this definition
encompasses the above and extends it to the Chicano society, the

community, in a genuine communal spirit. Perhaps the major difference between most Americans and Chicanos is that Chicanos are not individualistic.

THE STUDY OF SOCIAL EXCLUSION

A formal or informal policy of exclusion leaves most minorities little choice about how to react. They act to survive. Most attention has been focused on social stratification to explain not only the reactions to discrimination but also the causes and consequences of discrimination. The first example of this kind of attention was in the area of poverty. Some of the major causes of poverty include few resources; discrimination; the interaction of the social institutions in barring upward mobility; the subtle workings of status, power, and prestige; and life changes, which may include biological inheritance and the resistance of the dominant society to social change. Most social science approaches isolate factors such as lack of education, economics, and urbanization to explain poverty, but poverty is a multifaceted phenomenon. It is produced by the subtle, simultaneous workings of several factors in society.

Students of sociology frequently encounter textbooks that have chapters or sections on the nature of socialization, deviance, social control, social stratification, social institutions, and perhaps the future of society. This format has not changed much since the 1970s. Recently, textbooks have included chapters on racial-ethnic minorities, women, and other minority groups such as homosexuals. Where these chapters are placed in the textbook varies. Most are placed under a loosely defined category or heading "Social Inequality." While some authors have done a good job of articulating the issues, they often fail to integrate their own knowledge. They often give information in a manner that allows the student to memorize definitions and concepts, and pass the exam. They fail to teach critical thinking in an integrated, holistic manner. Thus, many students lack the ability to engage in holistic, critical thinking.

The newest scholarship in academe is in minority and women's studies, and it is holistic. It is, however, interdisciplinary, and it threatens traditional social scientists who have carved out areas of specialization in traditionally accepted disciplines. Most social scientists prefer not to change, not to relearn ways of thinking, and not to strongly criticize their ideology or their areas of specialization because this would require reconstructing departments, colleges, universities, their personal lives, and dominant social values. That, in turn, would require more training and the sharing of jobs and benefits with racial-ethnic minorities and women.

The truth is that society is not as open as most think, and that people do not have as much freedom as they think. Americans would like to believe that America is the land of opportunity, with freedom and justice for all, but some people are more free than others. It is not an accident that people of color are poor, and that women with children are the poorest. The social system, for the most part, "sets up" the poor to be poor, the middle income to be middle income, and the rich to be rich. It perpetuates itself.

There are various forms of social stratification. While some are economic, others have to do with other elements of society. Researchers have identified prestige as a factor. They have documented that people rate others according to occupation (Reiss et al. 1961). Duplication of this research has led to consistent findings since the late 1930s. It appears that people's opinions have not changed over that period. Physicians, college professors, and lawyers still rank the highest in prestige. Other ways in which society is stratified include age, emotional and physical ability, sexual preference, race, and gender. Unlike a caste system, in the United States people are not cemented into a class position. Social mobility is theoretically possible.

CHICANOS AND THE CLASS STRUCTURE

As stated before, Chicanos are represented at every level in society. Stereotypically, they are thought of as poor. Poverty, in spite of its bad reputation, is functional. The treatment of the poor serves as a warning to American workers. The consequences of not being the norm are negative; but labor pools of the poor are always available to provide cheap labor and additional workers. When fewer workers are needed, the poor move into the reserve labor pool. Poverty also makes jobs. Many people have jobs helping the poor. Social workers, welfare workers, educational and job counselors, food stamp personnel, and Medicaid and Medicare officers help poor people. Teachers, doctors, attorneys, nurses, politicians, business people, and many employers make money addressing the needs of the poor.

Poor people have little education and hold manual jobs with little prestige. Poor Chicanos are the janitors and garbage collectors of

society. Most are unskilled laborers. Chicano jobs are physically
demanding, dead-end, and dangerous. Chicanos tend to be migrant
workers, dishwashers, and domestics. Women have a high concentration in the service areas and are waitresses, laundry and garment
workers, department store clerks, and maids in hotels. Frequently
they are heads of households or are supplementing another income.
These people are grossly underpaid and have been called the working
poor. Although their work is socially necessary, it is never paid well.

The poor live in crowded, rundown, cheap housing. Few Chicanos
have become poor. Most were born into poverty. Like other poor
people, the Chicano poor are relatively invisible, segregated in ghettos, barrios, and deteriorating communities. They are ignored by
others and kept out of sight by freeways, factories, railroad yards,
industrial plants, laws, and social pressure.

It is ironic that at the same time poor individuals are invisible, they
have no privacy. Because they are forced to secure social services
from the government, they must reveal intimate elements of their
personal lives. This information is always available as data to be used
in budgeting and funding, in national, annual or biannual reports.
Further, the police are always in poor communities, constantly mon-
itoring behavior.

Most Americans blame the poor for their poverty. They do not
recognize the discriminatory tendency to use the poor as examples
of what happens to those who are not part of the norm in society.
Most drastically punished are those who choose not to conform and
those, like people of color, who cannot conform.

The working class has a slightly different life-style, but it also
consists of overcrowded, rundown homes and physical exhaustion.
For them, as for the poor, the American dream and all that sustains
it promise a better quality of life. The media uphold these working-
class dreams. For working-class youth, the major life objective is
marriage and work. Marriage promises independence and the hope
for a better life. Educational aspirations appear to be on the increase,
but the social structure and family pressure may push a young person
into early work responsibilities. These pressures, plus any dysfunctional coping skills, may further lower the life chances of working-
class youth. While middle-income youth are engaging in sports,
hobbies, homework, and dating, Chicano working-class youth are
working and/or married. Young men are frequently in dead-end
jobs, and young women are homemakers and mothers by the age

of 18 to 20. While still young, they are subjected to the stresses of paying bills and raising children.

During the economic recession of the early 1980s, many middle-class persons slid into the working and lower classes. The middle class encompasses white-collar workers and the professions. Chicanos who have climbed into this class act as role models for Chicanos in the lower classes. This class also acts as a buffer between the lower classes and the upper classes.

The upper class is very private compared with the middle class, which engages in some conspicuous consumption. It has been estimated that this affluent class consists of 1 to 3 percent of the population, but that it controls or owns 25 percent of the nation's wealth. These figures may be conservative.

For the most part these people inherit wealth. The poor and the middle class usually do not. The wealthy are a tightly knit group consisting of the old rich and the new rich. The old rich have had wealth for generations. The new rich acquired wealth only recently. There generally are few relationships between the two groups, although they sometimes cross paths. These people have much leisure time and may discreetly engage in social philanthropy. Chicano membership in this class is rare.

SEXISM IN SOCIETY

How racism permeates the society and sets up barriers to upward mobility for people of color has been discussed. Sexism exists in the same fashion. It functions to fixate a stratified social system. For women, the American dream is a little different than it is for men. Society socializes young girls to grow up with intentions to marry or otherwise link up with a male. Men are important social and economic assets in female lives. Women are not meant to enter directly into the labor market and thereby make a contribution. They are to stimulate it, indirectly, as consumers.

Society brainwashes women into thinking they are incomplete and can obtain social worth only if they have a dominant-group version of what is defined as a beautiful body, marriage, and children. For some women this has changed, but not for many. Female socialization (the process of learning culture) and the internalization of what has been learned sustain the artificial importance and dominance of men. It produces children, the future workers for the capitalist system, and it keeps women in the role of consumers and out of the competitive job market. Marriage, however, rarely brings all the status, power, and prestige that women think it will bring. Fantasies and dreams typically remain unrealized, not only for women but also for men. Nevertheless, people remain addicted to the American dream, its teaching, its assumptions, and its promises of a good life if people adhere to the social norms.

American gender roles are based on the socialization of people according to gender. Gender roles are the behaviors, rights, and responsibilities assigned to each sex in a culture. While women and men are different, they are also very much the same. More often than not, male-female differences are rooted more in degrees of power and perception than in reality. American culture has created very great differernces in the lives of women and men. Fundamentally, social scientists are more interested in understanding power structures, status, and other social variables. This interest, however, did not arise until women entered the field.

Mexican American and black women are also part of this discussion. They have made astonishing contributions concerning women and the lives of people of color. Their major contribution has been an insight into the "double whammy." It was these women who made it clear to white women, social scientists, and society in general that they were doubly discriminated against. They were victimized for being people of color and for being female. Additionally, some suffered because of their lower-class status.

CHICANA CULTURAL IMPORTANCE

Although American gender roles are changing, perhaps Mexican Americans are still adhering more to traditional sex roles. This is not to point an accusing finger while charging Mexican American men with sexism. It is true that, like other U.S. cultures, this population has strong social prescriptions; but other factors intervene. Mexican Americans need strongly defined gender roles in order to sustain a coping and upwardly mobile standard of life in two very strong cultures. In Chicano culture, people depend on one another. Thus, women must depend more on men and men must depend more on women. This is not sexism; it is survival. Both sexes depend on marriage to provide status and protection from the harsh, sometimes violent, realities of minority status. The white population does not have to contend with this multifaceted concern.

It is still a fact that Anglo women in America tend to earn roughly 63 cents for every dollar earned by males. Chicanas earn less than Anglo females. Extremely low Chicano earnings call for most couples to work to (barely) meet personal needs and the needs of their families.

Women are strong in Chicano culture. They are strong as cultural and decision-making symbols, and they are strong physically. Cultural and historical social conditions have demanded that both males and females work hard. Both men and women value home life. Women are not hesitant to work alongside men in maintaining their home. After working long hours during the week (longer than most white men for the same pay), Chicano men do not hesitate to work around their homes. Increasingly, more men are involved in child rearing.

Chicanos are predominantly working class. They have an internalized work ethic somewhat similar to the dominant work ethic. Their common experience as an ethnic minority has oppressed these hard-working people. This experience often defuses the gender role issue so important in Anglo society.

Sexism exists in Chicano society. Men have adopted and have sustained preferential positions and treatment. To some extent this has always existed, but the more urbanized and the more assimilated the Chicanos become, the more the power differential between women and men increases. For U.S.-born Chicanos, the form that this has taken recently is more American than Mexican.

At birth Chicano females and males start out the same. They subsequently experience different roles, but it is life chances that become important. Because females bear children, men do not have to endure being subjected to racist and sexist health standards, practices, and systems in delivery rooms. Chicanas have more children than white women, and therefore are subjected to delivery rooms more frequently than are Anglo women.

Chicano men, like white men, feel women are responsible for birth control and should have primary responsibility for raising children. This opinion is based more on the cultural importance of women than it is rooted in releasing themselves from child-rearing responsibility. On the surface this appears as blatant sexism, but it is not. The indigenous part of Chicano culture supports matriarchy, and women maintain strong cultural roles. In addition, there has been an attempt to treat the Chicano male as black men have been treated. Discrimination works to emasculate them, to make them feel inferior. This tactic, however, has not taken a strong hold in Chicano society, and most Chicano males have strong female role models.

Perhaps the most important factor is life itself. Sexist tendencies manifest themselves in terms of life expectancies. White men have a shorter life expectancy than white women even though they experience preferential treatment. They live to an average age of 70.8 years, while white women live to roughly 78.2 years. The shorter life span for white males is probably attributable to the stress inherent in male culture: upward mobility, competition, individualism, sustaining the status quo, and practicing sexism and racism.

Chicano men do not live as long as white men, and Chicanas do not live as long as white women. Chicano women and men die earlier because of inadequate health care and the added stresses of the victimization of racism and sexism. Anglos, especially Anglo woman, are not subjected to social victimization to the same degree and in the same manner as are Chicanos. The study of death rates is certainly in need of more research.

A review of the literature on Chicanas and the Chicano family will reveal a stereotyped picture of a woman in the role of wife and mother: docile, passive, uncomplaining, all-suffering, all-forgiving, and hard-working (Melville 1980). She is presented as the victim of a violent, unfaithful male. Perhaps this is how people would like to perceive her, and perhaps some of the stereotypes have been forced to become elements of truth. However, Chicanas are not as they are presented to be. They are not more abused than white women, nor are they endowed with the animalistic qualities projected by racism and sexism.

MULTI-SEGMENTED SOCIAL SYSTEM

Members of the Chicano community and Chicano scholars have recognized a dual system since the Anglo takeover in 1846. The dual system recognizes that prior to 1848 there was one set of unwritten, often unspoken, rules for the white segment of the world and a second for the people of color. In the case of the American Chicano this perspective should be extended to include at least three value systems: one for women, one for the poor, and one for people of color.

On the surface Americans have the same formal standing, but informally people of color and women have a secondary and tertiary standing. Women of color often make up the least-valued segment in a multi-segmented social system that operates at several latent and manifest levels. The levels include different rules, expectations, statuses, power, and prestige for white men, white women, the poor, men of color, and women of color. Specific jobs and social opportunities are available to each, with the higher-status, higher-prestige, and higher-income positions given to Anglo men. Society has put much time and energy into denying this, but it exists.

In the 1960s Americans acted shocked to discover poverty and racism in their country. Michael Harrington (1963) opened the discussion of poverty in America for sociologists. America, through Lyndon B. Johnson's War on Poverty and the efforts of the civil rights movement, became aware of the existence of Chicanos in the nation. The fact that this group existed in a historically downtrodden position was a surprise to most. Chicanos had been a well-kept secret.

With the study of the Chicano has come the realization that Anglos cannot exist in privilege unless people of color exist without privilege. The multi-segmented system exerts a push-pull strain to make it all work well. The objective and the consequences of the cumulative effort are different for each segment. The minority works much harder to live out its limited life chances, while the Anglos work to keep themselves comfortable.

The multi-segmented system is perhaps best seen at work in the criminal justice system. Being a person of color means increased chances of encountering the law, being sent to prison, and appearing on death row, especially if a white person is killed as part of a crime. White people with wealth will have fewer of these experiences. When they make contact with law officials, the reason for contact and the duration of the experience will be different. The poorer person will, generally, have an experience as a suspect or as an offender more frequently than as a person needing protection, information, or assistance. It has been documented that the poor and the people of color receive more guilty verdicts, longer sentences, and higher fines in the criminal justice system. More people of color go to jail. These findings are directly dependent on at least three factors: the money a person has to hire a competent attorney, the network of infuential persons who can assist, and what that person represents to the establishment (the social value and worth of the individual or the social group the individual respresents).

SUMMARY

Chicanos feel the need to make corrections in the criminal justice system and in the governing of American society. Many people of color do not trust the government to address their concerns, and some do not view government officials as a body with final responsibility for social decisions. The belief in nonresponsive government is based on experiences in Chicano history, the violation of the Treaty of Guadalupe Hidalgo, and how the government has formulated racist, sexist policies that negatively effect Chicanos and people in other Spanish-speaking, Third World countries. Some people, including Chicanos, believe that a policy on the dissolution of racism and sexism can be legislated; others believe it cannot.

Racism and sexism have become American cultural characteristics. They are embedded in the social fabric. Change in the social stratification has to be approached from within the several social institutions simultaneously and integrated into family life, religion, politics, education, the law, the health system, and economics. Of course, this assumes that class, race, and gender equality are desired outcomes, and that inequality is neither desired nor functional. The truth is, many people gain from social stratification and silently support multi-segmentation.

REFERENCES

Almaguer, Tomas. 1975. "Toward the Study of Chicano Colonialism." *Aztlan: Chicano Journal of the Social Sciences and the Arts,* 2: 7–21.

Barrera, Mario. 1979. *Race and Class in the Southwest.* South Bend, IN: University of Notre Dame Press.

Blea, Irene I. 1981. "An Analysis of Mexican American Homemaking." Paper presented at 1977 National Association of Chicano Studies Conference, Claremont, CA.

———. 1981b. "Bessemer: A Sociological Perspective of a Chicano Barrio." Ph.D. diss., University of Colorado, Boulder.

———. 1988. *Bessemer.* New York: AMS Press.

Engels, Friedrich, ed. 1967. *Capital,* by Karl Marx. 3 vols. New York: International Publishers.

García, Mario. 1981. *Desert Immigrants: The Mexicans of El Paso, 1880–1920.* New Haven: Yale University Press.

Gerth, H. H., and C. Wright Mills. 1946. *From Max Weber: Essays in Sociology.* New York: Oxford University Press.

Harrington, Michael. 1963. *The Other America: Poverty in the United States.* Baltimore: Penguin.

Melville, Margaritta B. 1980. *Twice a Minority.* St. Louis: C. V. Mosby.

Mirande, Alfredo. 1985. *The Chicano Experience.* South Bend, IN: University of Notre Dame Press.

Muñoz, Carlos, Jr. 1972. "The Politics of Urban Protest: A Model of Political Analysis." Ph.D. diss., Claremont College, Graduate School of Government.

Reiss, Albert J., O. D. Duncan, Paul K. Hatt, and C. C. North. 1961. *Occupations and Social Status.* Glencoe, IL: Free Press.

Rose, Peter. 1981. *They and We: Racial and Ethnic Relations in the United States.* 3rd ed. New York: Random House.

Terkel, Studs. 1974. *Working.* New York: Pantheon Books.

United States Bureau of the Census. 1985. *Persons of Spanish Origin in the United States.* Current Population Reports Series, P. 20, no. 310 (July) and no. 328 (August). Washington, DC: U.S. Government Printing Office.

3
Social-Cultural Profile

INTRODUCTION

The factors that most strongly define culture and to which culture gives definition are values, norms, symbols, and communication forms. Cultural productions are the things that culture produces and manifests in art, poetry, music, religion, and other social institutions, such as education and the family. These factors deal with hope, fears, objectives of life, and death. In Chicano culture they manifest as family structure and family relationships; a high value for cleanliness, marriage, children, education, the elderly, religion, and spirituality; interaction between the sexes; days of significance; and the need for social change.

Perhaps the biggest Chicano fear is that children will absorb dominant American values and that talented people with resources will be lost to the community and to their families. Perhaps the biggest hope is that the community will become economically stable, that racism will end, and that Chicanos will be allowed to participate fully in the ongoing society without having to give up their culture.

Culture is important to Chicanos because it is the thing that sustains people. It gives them shared knowledge and direction for meeting their objectives. Without this, people are empty, lost, and confused. Individuals may become disoriented and depressed, even suicidal, without cultural references. The person without culture is not rooted and has a difficult time relating. Populations in secondary social positions especially need culture for insulation against oppressive forces. For the Chicanos this is extraordinarily important because Chicano culture has systematically been devalued by the dominant society. Chicanos have been placed in a position of needing and wanting their culture, having it devalued, and having to defend against strong depreciation tactics by the dominant culture.

Culture includes rites of passage, those times in a person's life that are symbolic of having passed from one status to another. In Chicano culture these include birth, baptism, beginning school, confirmation, *quincinera* (a 15-year-old coming-out fiesta) for some females, marriage, and death.

THE ROLE OF RELIGION

Before and while going to school, most young Chicanos who grow up in a Chicano community have much experience with the Catholic religion. Alfredo Mirande (1985) does an outstanding job of presenting the function of the Catholic Church in Chicano history. I desire to outline the structure and function, and the nature of Catholicism, in Chicano culture.

A sociological definition of religion states that religion is a social institution. It is a social structure built around widely shared and accepted beliefs, procedures, norms, and values. Social institutions endure because they meet the needs of people. They are slow to change and are frequently linked to other institutions. For example, religion is linked to the family, economics, politics, and health.

Religion is a system of shared beliefs and practices built around the idea of supernatural forces that link the individual to a much greater power. Supernatural forces are used as an explanation for that which is known and that which is unknown. Characteristic of the manifestation of religion are the notions of God or gods, the spirit life, the afterlife, salvation, and damnation. Religion as it is known in America involves prayer and ritual.

Culture, society, and social relationships affect religion, and religion affects the society, culture, and the social relationships of individuals. Religion is a fundamental feature of society, and it is a fundamental feature in Chicano culture. It assists in defining the Chicano in relationship to earth, to heaven, to hell, to purgatory, to people, and to supernatural beings. Religion and spirituality have helped Chicanos understand their place in the universe, but they have not done this through the teachings of the Catholic Church alone. Chicano culture has elements of indigenous religions and other cultural ways of interaction.

Chicanos have come to know Catholicism via the Catholic Church, which is highly bureaucratic and consistent with dominant norms and values. There are hierarchical positions, areas of specialization, official creeds, and formal training required for participation. Most Chicanos have inherited this ongoing structure because they were born into the Catholic faith. The church did not have to work to convert them. Chicanos, for the most part, were socialized into participating in and internalizing the church's doctrine. This doctrine excludes indigenous religion and interprets it as the work of the uncivilized and even of the devil.

The church and urbanization, plus increased contact with the dominant Anglo culture, have changed traditional Mexican American religious practices. The mixture of Spanish and Indian society, however, is still evident throughout the Southwest in practices more commonly known as folk religion, folk medicine, and folkways. Southwest residents are very able to discuss their Indian and Spanish traditions of child rearing, Penitentes, the Virgin of Guadalupe, *brujería* (a spiritual practice frequently linked to witchcraft) and *curanderismo* (a form of holistic health and healing), baptism, confirmation, and beliefs in ghosts or spirits. It should be understood that involved in this complex system of health and healing the supernatural, and good and evil, form an element of religion that constitutes for the Chicano a world view somewhat consistent with, yet different from, the Anglo view. Increasingly these elements have been violated, discredited, challenged, diluted, and separated, and have been channeled into institutions rooted in the dominant society.

My own research on Bessemer (1988) revealed that although a great number of people said they were Catholic, they did not always practice their religion by going to church every Sunday and on holy days of obligation, saying daily prayers, or otherwise behaving as Catholics. Some people had home altars and images of the saints. They used their Catholic religion at the same time they used Indian herbs and prayer in medicine. Those who had chosen to attend church and fully live Catholic lives sought to make their religion more relevant to themselves by having music, prayers, and readings in Spanish. Throughout the United States, increasingly there are more Mexican American laypersons involved in the church. Mariachi masses are common. Also common and indicative of the religious commitment of some are the statues of the Virgin and Jesus exhibited in the yards and in the homes of many citizens. Many people have patron saints to whom they pray for assistance, good health, good jobs, racial justice, and peace in the world. Home altars at which people light candles and pray to the saints for guidance, assistance, and deliverance are very much an Indian and a Spanish tradition. Religion enables individuals to make sense of their world. It guides them in times of crisis.

In the Chicano community, religion is an intimate element of daily life, providing a vehicle for socializing by bringing family and friends together on a serious spiritual note. It plays its first role in the practice of baptism. A major element of this ritual is the very personal parental selection of *compadres* and *comadres,* male and female godparents or sponsors. Participation in the ritual establishes a relationship between the child and the male and female sponsors. The relationship is referred to by the child as *padrinos.* The female sponsor or godparent is called *madrina.* Equally important is the relationship between the parents and the male and female sponsors. To non-Spanish speakers the terms become confusing when *compadres* and *comadres* also play a role in marriage and the extended family structure. It does not make sense to them that so many people are involved, especially during times of illness and personal crisis.

MARRIAGE AND FEMALE-MALE RELATIONSHIPS

Like most Americans, Chicanos usually marry people of the opposite sex and of the same race. Because keeping the culture intact is important, there is pressure to marry within the same ethnic group. Other American populations have been known to have the same preference. It is not uncommon for Italian families, for example, to insist that their children marry Italians. Many Anglos also resist intermarriage.

In America people marry primarily because they fall in love with people who attract them. What attracts, however, is strongly dictated by the norms and roles of the culture, the society; there is strong social influence upon us to marry people who are like us. Love is a relatively new idea as a basis for marriage, and we still have in our society remnants of the time when marriage was arranged on the basis of landholdings, power, status, and prestige. Few people would admit that they marry for some of these social reasons, and they use love as the vehicle to mask some subtle, unconscious, but strong considerations.

From a theoretical perspective, the workings of racism and sexism may perhaps be seen more clearly when we observe intermarriage. I will proceed on the assumption that groups and people are given social worth. The most valued and powerful social group is the dominant group—the white group we call Anglos. The most valued and powerful persons are the white men, then the white females. Social institutions, particularly the media, have ensured this in many ways. Men of color have less value than white females, and a minority female of color is the least valued of all. Thus, when a white man marries, he always marries someone of lower social value. This helps cement his superiority. When a minority man marries, he has a choice of marrying a minority female (marrying down) or marrying a white female (marrying up). Some men of color can marry up because the male-dominated character of recent society has ensured men of special privileges.

When white women decide to marry, they also have a choice. They can marry up (marry white males) and be in a secondary position, or they can marry down (marry a minority male) and be more powerful. A minority female, however, does not have this choice. She is at the lowest end of the social racial-sexual scale and can only marry up.

This model of course excludes homosexual and lesbian relationships. Research into the nature of interracial homosexual and lesbian relationships is certainly warranted. My conclusion is that white females and minority males appear to have the greatest choice in mate selection. This appearance can be a benefit when the partners are healthy in their approach to racism and sexism.

NEGATIVE GENDER RELATIONSHIPS

A quick review of the feminist literature very rapidly reveals that white males have received much social reward on the basis of their whiteness and their maleness. Women have had to learn to live and create in a secondary position, and they have learned to do this very well. Nevertheless, they have suffered. Sometimes women engage in male-female relationships in ways that are not functional, and

Chicanas are among them. These dysfunctional relationships have hurt women who often become victims of "blaming the victim" theoretical models and personal perspectives.

Often women place too much blame on themselves for making bad choices. An interesting insight into women who make bad choices emerges in Robin Norwood's *Women Who Love too Much* (1985). Her fundamental premise is that some women become addicted to relationships. Their desire to love, their yearning, their actual loving is a form of addiction. Love is especially important to Chicanas, who are reared with a high regard for children, marriage, and families with clean, healthy homes. Many of these women get into dependent relationships, especially if they come from dysfunctional families and were damaged in childhood. These women align themselves with men who are physically or emotionally unavailable, or otherwise unable to love. Women who love too much think they can change their unloving man. They feel that if only they could make him happy, their relationship would be fine. They try to make the relationship work, but it cannot. They are in a sick relationship.

Often the male will psychologically and physically abuse this female and convince her that it is her fault he is not happy, or he blames her for his addiction to alcohol, drugs, sports, or work. His tactic is to mask the real problem. Why are these women this way? Norwood notes that her contentions are limited to white women, but she does shed some light on the nature of women's social oppression by stating that women are socialized to nurture. They carry this nurturing characteristic into relationships with men who expect to be nurtured. In part the trap is social. Men addict externally on drugs, alcohol, sports, and work, but they addict more impersonally. Some men addict to other people, but this is more a feminine trait. Women respond to hurting individuals with sympathy and understanding, and they seek men upon whom they can practice what they have been taught.

Females, according to Norwood, learn dysfunctional norms in families where their childhood needs were not met, where roles were rigid and communication was limited to statements that fit the female role in that family. These women are not able to express their full range of wants, needs, and feelings, and have limited themselves to roles that accommodate others. This is the social norm for American women, including most Chicanas.

But Norwood places too much emphasis on sexism and the family.

Racism, the media, religion, politics, economics, and education support gender roles. When discussing the roles of Chicanos and Chicanas, racism becomes a fundamental part of the discussion because it affects the arena of choice. Choice becomes limited, particularly for the Chicana.

Flexibility in choice, resources, the opportunity to communicate the need for alternative roles, wants, needs, and feelings are healthy things. Women are denied this. People of color are denied this. Women of color are in the worst social position to experience healthy social lives. The person in a position to be the most socially healthy is the white male because he has the most flexibility, the most resources; yet he has his own set of problems with his own sex role, sexism, and racism.

Norwood goes on to note that in a dysfunctional family, major aspects of reality are denied to the female. She is shielded from the truth. This is why sex roles remain rigid. Dysfunctional families also do not adapt to changing times. Many men have not adapted to the changing roles of women. They seek to keep the social roles rigid because they fear losing privilege. I maintain that men—expressly minority men—have nothing to fear except their own liberation, and that it is in their own interest to practice feminism. Unfortunately, the word "feminism" is alienating to many men. To some men it means either "bra-burning women libbers" or to be "womanlike." Contemporary men are repelled by both the stereotyped "radical" female behavior and by the pink, powdery softness of women dependent on their femininity. Therefore, I propose that feminists find a genderless term for feminism. "Egalitarian" is a term that denotes the inclusion of men and women with feminist convictions, convictions that were once at the heart of Chicano culture. This term should make clear that the person being labeled is one who respects and supports equal rights for all human beings. Feminists and egalitarians need not only to say this but also to live their lives accordingly.

I further suggest that the term be one that implies an end to discrimination against racial and ethnic minorities, the aged, the young, the poor, and the physically and mentally impaired. For the sake of promoting discussion, I propose the word "egalitarianist," and note that some differences between men and women complement the life cycle. However, artificial differences complicate it and produce unnecessary stress. Men, including Chicano men, have taken advantage of the privileges accorded them by virtue of their male sex, and in the process they have negated their responsibility to community. Men have a responsibility for making the life cycle less stressful. Yet most men do not assume or accept this responsibility. Some women, including chicanas, have assumed the responsibility for themselves as well as for their men.

Males have not come forth to openly discuss the fact that sexism oppresses them. The very nature of the socially defined male sex role leads men to commit suicide more often, to become victimized by drug and alcohol addiction. Men have more ulcers, more heart attacks, are more likely to be criminals, to be violent, and to die violent deaths. They suffer more alienation, fear of war, and lack of social skills. It is in the male interest to seek and participate in open discussion of male discrimination through social expectations based on the fact that they were born male.

For the majority of males in America, this sense of power is false and economic. For Chicano men it is mostly false. Men have to realize that they hold false power, status, and prestige. The notion that they possess these social attributes keeps them participating in a system that is oppressive to themselves and to others. Currently their justification for participation is that at least they have more resources than women. In reality, if sex roles were relaxed, the vast majority of men would live a less stressful life, with fewer suicides, less alcoholism, less drug addiction, and fewer ulcers. Men would not die of heart attacks at the age of 45. Going to war would be debatable because violent behavior to settle differences would not be the sole alternative.

However, in spite of what men stand to gain, very few men will enter into a discussion about themselves as liberated men. With the change I propose, men and women would experience the end of internalized discriminatory behavior that places them in contradictory and conflicting dichotomies that sometimes function without an awareness of the oppression in our social system. Thus, if men want to live longer, want to live in peace, want to rid their society of discrimination, and want to lead a less stressful life, they will become egalitarianists and behave in a manner that is supportive of the feminist and minority movements.

Many still believe they need someone to take care of them and have forgotten that it is they who are the caretakers. Perhaps this desire exists because the burden of caretaking is too heavy. Some women, however, feel that there is little need for men to invest in feminism. Equality is threatening to those women. Also threatening to them is having to take care of themselves and be responsible for themselves. The women who speak against feminism prefer to remain sheltered from economic and political realities and social stress. They prefer to let men bear the brunt of such visible stress, and in this preference they contribute to the manipulation of sex roles that results in male oppression that also oppresses women. This is a very dangerous, inhumane tactic.

A perception against this view is not new to Chicano culture. This is why some Chicanas do not abandon their men in struggling for liberation. A renewed commitment to what once worked very well for Chicanos—egalitarianism between the sexes—is something that Chicana feminists continue to strive for.

SIGNIFICANT CULTURAL OBSERVANCES

Birth, family relationships, death, and the Catholic Church are very closely related. They have spiritual components. Many Chicanos believe that church participation serves to ensure passage into heaven. Even those who have not been observant Catholics are given a mass and religious burial. The rituals allow individuals to understand and cope with the crisis they face. The religious tradition functions as a prescribed way of doing things. It affords individuals freedom from having to make major decisions at an emotional time. The contemporary Catholic tradition has come a long way from the traditional *velorio*. This early tradition included a three-day vigil over the unembalmed body in the home of one of the deceased's loved ones.

As in child rearing, women are very important in the death and dying phase of life. Women inform other family members of who is to be contacted about a death. They assign sleeping quarters, cook meals, and greet guests. They are also the first to enter the church and keep the children quiet.

Present at all Hispanic funerals are a number of children. According to many priests, more Mexican American children attend funerals than do children in any other ethnic group, except perhaps for Italians. Chicano children are allowed to move about, to look at and touch the body at funerals. It is felt that this is healthy, for it teaches children to cope with and accept death. Through this practice children learn that death is part of life and that it is not to be feared. This belief is very Native American and especially characteristic of the Pueblo people.

Easter has always been an important religious holiday. The Easter season begins on Ash Wednesday, 40 days and 40 nights before Easter. On Ash Wednesday the faithful go to church and the priest traces a small cross of ashes on their forehead. In northern New Mexico and southern Colorado the focus is on the passion of Christ, and is firmly rooted in the tradition of the Hermanos Penitentes. This brotherhood is known for the use of flagellation as a means of expiating sins and reliving the torment of Christ during his final days on earth. The Penitente brotherhood is a living brotherhood. Families familiar with the tradition live throughout the United States.

Women are generally in charge of teaching children about cultural ways, especially religious holidays and death. Many Americans have limited the observance of Easter to gathering eggs and having dinner on Easter Sunday. There is the opinion that, like Christmas, Easter has become very commercial.

For many Chicanos, Easter means going to church and having a large family meal. Traditional Easter foods include *panocha,* a wheat pudding. In some areas it is prepared and eaten only during Holy Week. Observance of Easter week begins on Wednesday of Holy Week with fasting and prayer. Abstention from meat is required. In many Chicano homes Lenten food is prepared by the women. *Lentejas* (lentils), *posole* (hominy and meat stew), and *torta huevo* (egg patties simmered in mild chile sauce) are bland foods suited for a fasting stomach but very high in protein. They contain no meat and were fed to Penitentes after long hours of fasting and flagellation. Many Chicanos still give up certain activities and food for the entire duration of Lent. Purchasing an Easter outfit is falling in importance, and in general Easter is truly a holy day. The more devoted keep relative silence and eat no meat during Easter week. Every day, beginning on Wednesday, they attend mass to pray the Stations of the Cross, and they spend all afternoon on Good Friday in church. There was a time where barrio banks and stores closed from one until three o'clock in the afternoon. A few closed for the entire afternoon. This no longer is the case. On Easter Sunday, Chicano Catholics receive Communion.

Christmas is not as holy a day as Easter, and Chicano practices are fairly consistent with Christmas practices of other Americans. It is a family season of purchases and festivity involving some drinking, dressing up, and dancing. It is a time for exchanging gifts, and most of all it is a time for family. Some people decorate their homes with colored lights and nativity scenes. Most have Christmas trees, and many have much to eat. On Christmas Eve community members attend midnight mass, the *misa del gallo*. Some open gifts and eat festive foods, and do not attend the mass; others open gifts and eat after mass. Others wait until morning to open gifts. Special emphasis is placed on the mother's gift. Some Chicanos attend mass on Christmas day, but a primary focus is on the family's gathering for the opening of gifts and the Christmas dinner of tamales, ham, or turkey. The holidays extend to New Year's Day and generally appear to be a good time for all who have family. As with other Americans, for those who have no family or whose family is characterized by conflict or poverty, this may be an unhappy time. Unresolved family issues surface and the contradiction of Christmas arises, mixed with food and drink.

There are other important holidays for the community that are both spiritual and social. There are days commemorating the saints and birthdays. There are also church festivals. The most obvious aspect of the church festival is the carnival, which includes food and game booths. Prior to the opening of the carnival, there is a mass and a religious procession featuring the honored saint. Church carnivals, birthdays, weddings, and funerals are excellent opportunities for socializing and catching up on what has happened to people and their families.

The Catholic Church is still very strictly male-dominated. For this reason very few women have left the church. But Chicanos have increasingly deviated from the Catholic Church. The recent move away from the church is rooted in the Chicano movement of the 1960s. It was during the latter part of the decade that activists began to criticize the church as exploiting Chicanos by taking what little money they had and giving little in return. The church was accused of making Chicanos accept oppressive social conditions by promising a better life after death. This hindered social change. On the other hand, some Chicano Catholics and priests maintain that faith, belief in the Lord and an afterlife, has given the Chicanos spiritual nourishment and motivation on earth.

Many Chicanos have converted to other religions. Some of these new religions are very fundamental. Those who have converted cite contradictions in the Catholic Church and faith as major reasons.

Other reasons include too much ceremony and ritual in the church. The priest plays too great a role and generally speaks English. This keeps people from forming and maintaining a direct relationship with God. The priests and the church structure interfere too much with what people want to do.

The fundamentalist religions hold entire services in Spanish. They have Spanish prayers, teachings, and songs. People are an integral part of the services, not just an adornment. These religions are also more expressive. People can testify before the group. They can ask questions, clap hands to music, cry, and pray out loud. Much dancing and joy in knowing that the Lord exists are exhibited. People offer to pray for one another. They ask for prayer, and they touch and visit one another. In alternative churches, women have found new roles and new power. There they are called sisters, and the men are their brothers. There is little or no hierarchy. Women testify at microphones, they lead prayers, preach, cite passages from the Bible, sing, and generally feel more fully a part of the services. In the non-Catholic churches social-political awareness is manifested in the testimonies. This is very unlike the Catholic Church practices.

CULTURAL VALUES

Emile Durkheim (1915) wrote that religion is necessary for a society because it integrates values. This is crucial because it sustains social cohesion. The Chicano people have internalized religion for these reasons.

Spirituality does not always mean religion, but a fundamental belief about the nature of the intangible world. Chicanos sometimes voice opinions that the Anglos have become rather spiritually void persons. In having internalized some American values, some Chicanos also have lost spirituality.

Religious spirituality contributes to ideology, a set of ideas, norms, and values that support and rationalize the existing social structure. Dominant religion and ideology tell social participants that social arrangements are adequate, that they are how they should be: natural. For the most part, ideologies become cemented during the socialization process, which never ends. A person continues learning social roles, norms, and behaviors throughout life. Ideologies can change, but unless a person has an intense desire or a significant event occurs, most people never think about what they have learned by being a social participant. They take their knowledge for granted, as actual and as true. Thus, they have little motivation to change and may live under false consciousness, thiking that what they believe is true.

Like other people, Chicanos do not think much about their own church history and the nature of the historical roots of their faith. Some are unaware of their indigenous spiritual ancestors. They have come to feel ashamed of being Indian, and they frequently discriminate against their indigenous history.

Church activists call for a Chicano liberation theology. They draw attention to the wealth of the church and the poverty of the Chicanos who helped build that wealth. Church activists insist that the church go past providing pastoral care and that, in addition to its noncontroversial activities in adoption, family counseling, and feeding and lodging the poor, it lift the burden of racial oppression from its marble floors and advance the cause of liberating the Chicano from the clutches of a dominant white society. The relief of oppression is the focus of two important days in Chicano existence: the Cinco de Mayo (May 5) and Dieciseis de Septiembre (September 16). These are days of prayer and celebration of independence and peaceful existence. Ironically, they are also days when Chicano gatherings are most likely to encounter police conflict. These days are also a celebration of ethnicity.

THE ROLE OF ETHNICITY

Many factors shape the human experience. It is in the study of the Chicano elderly that one gains significant insight into life as a Chicano in America. Some factors to be considered in the study of ethnicity are sex, country of origin, socioeconomic status, life span or longevity, life chances, color, and the ethnic support network. Contemporary social science study of the elderly Hispanic has focused upon whether race or ethnicity would increase or decrease eligibility for and access to social services. This research focus has led to the understanding of the senior Chicano in terms of those things held in common with all elderly, but it also has articulated those things held in common with other Chicano people.

The gerontological focus reviews the special needs of the older Chicano. Lacking in emphasis is what the elderly contribute to America and how the Chicanos specifically make contributions. A review of the literature quickly reveals that they are poorer than older Anglos

(Gelford 1982). They are more dependent on public benefits but may be least able to obtain them. They also may not live long enough to receive full social benefits. They are more susceptible to consumer abuse, and they suffer significantly from the legacy of racial discrimination. The women are highly victimized by sexism, a situation that typically is exacerbated by entering elder status.

Michael Gilfix (1977) states that poverty is without a doubt the leading factor creating a visible difference between all minority seniors and Anglo seniors. Whereas Anglos become poor in their old age, Chicanos suffer a far less perceptible decline in income. I contend that older Chicanos do not see themselves as poorer because they have always been poor, and that they place more emphasis on the social quality of their lives than they do on material aspects. Social relationships in their old age are of primary concern, although money is of course a necessity.

Most older Chicanos look forward to receiving Social Security benefits, but the receipt of such benefits displays racial/ethnic disparities. For example, more Chicanos than Anglos depend on Social Security benefits as their only source of income, but more Anglos than Chicanos receive Social Security benefits. Many Chicanos cannot obtain "insured status" because so many of their employers do not properly report all earnings. In addition, racial discrimination in employment and lower earnings result in lower benefits. Simultaneously, many minority seniors do not apply for other income-support benefits, such as Supplemental Security Income, because they do not know that they exist, or because they are reluctant to interact with intimidating bureaucracies, or because of what is perceived as disrespect. Some individuals are unsure of their resident status or are in the country without documentation, and fear deportation.

Chicano elders are further characterized by low-quality housing and health care. They, like other Chicanos, use natural networks to learn about opportunities. When information is needed, the elders question family, friends, neighbors, or other trusted individuals. Those people feel free to give the seniors suggestions. Assisting a Chicano elder usually means more than sharing information. It means physically being with the individual, helping the older person help himself/herself, linking the person with another trusted individual inside the system, or referring and introducing the person to someone trusted who knows another trusted person (Valle 1979). This mode of operation may be seen by the outsider as dependency. It is not.

It is a communal cultural way of obtaining information and securing services, and it is generally used by the population.

In studying elderly Mexican Americans, Deborah Newquist (1977) discovered that conducting research in minority communities uncovered some ethical questions that social scientists have failed to address: the ethics of bringing something of value to the community in return for valuable information. The issues of ethics and accountability are viewed differently by researchers and members of the community. Reciprocity, fair exchange without attached monetary value, is a cultural expectation. In Chicano culture one gives, not repays, a visit with a visit, a kindness with a kindness. Younger people are expected to defer to adults, particularly to seniors. Academics do not want to engage in this exchange or in this deference. They would prefer to continue using their ivory tower approach to studying the minority community. The community knows this, and basically distrusts researchers because they never give anything back. As long as insensitive researchers continue such conduct, Chicanos will tell them what they think the researchers want to hear and will continue to give false information. Many are choosing not to cooperate at all.

Some misleading conclusions have been drawn about the elderly, conclusions that affect the study of Chicanos in general. A commonly held stereotype is that the elderly are firmly supported by their strong nuclear families and their extended family networks. Newquist found that this is true in a special way. The family is definitely a resource in terms of social and emotional support, but because of its social and historical experience, it does not tend to be as strong a service provider. In fact, older Chicanos do not expect much from their family, and anticipate even less than do older Anglos. Newquist's work also documented that a lifetime of discrimination and survival has made minorities more adaptive, resourceful, and able to cope. This is linked to my contention that coping mechanisms do exist and that they are an area deserving more study. An area of needed concentration is the role of ethnicity as a coping mechanism. It acts as a source of continuity. Minorities experience much more social change or crisis due to social-historical conditions in the United States. The one thing that stays constant is their ethnicity. This is an important factor, in light of the importance of continuity of life patterns in the wellbeing of the total person. Cultural background certainly lends the elder Chicanos strength and support.

Certainly an issue attached to the quality of life is aging and what constitutes it. For many people aging is simple. One birthday follows another until old age. For social scientists aging is not as simplistic. There is a relationship between chronological age and social expectations, roles, norms, and perceptions. This relationship is also culturally relevant. In Chicano culture social influence increases with age. Seniors are the authorities on values and culture, for example. In a true Chicano experience, seniors lend direction to the future. However, as the population grows more sophisticated in urban living and internalizes Anglo perspectives, they relegate the elders' expertise to an area of folklore, an area that to some extent lacks legitimacy. Thus, the seniors are displaced from participating in the real aspects of life.

Because the "baby boom" generation is getting older, there is more attention being paid to aging. Attention to the older minority has been significant but limited to reports. In 1970, the U.S. Bureau of the Census reported that Native Americans and Mexican Americans had a life expectancy of less than 60 years. In 1980, the life expectancy was higher, especially for women. In 1971, the White House Conference on Aging gave special attention to the needs and circumstances of the aging of older minority people. At this conference, common concern for a nonchronological definition of aging was voiced. The conventional chronological definition, while it was standardized and convenient, inherently discriminated against the elderly because, socially and mentally, they aged faster.

The concept of functional age states that individuals age at different rates and that an estimate of an individual's age has dimensions that are mentally constructed. In layperson's terms, some people mature faster than others. Because Chicanos endure more social stress, they age faster. Aging also requires an integration of much knowledge and an acceptance of reality: knowledge about two cultures and two social systems that have continuously been in conflict. This stimulates mental activity or depression. No test has yet fully measured my contention. Existing measurement instruments are inadequate. Perhaps the closest related research has been conducted in the area of social aging.

Social age uses functional age as a base to identify psychological variables in its measurement. Some factors considered are abilities, personality, and self-concept. An integration or synthesis of the two concepts and the emergence of social-psychological definition might be the most productive. A new definition would bring immediate relief to minorities. They would immediately be affected by the retirement and eligibility age of 65 for Social Security. This arbitrary retirement age has worked against older Chicanos ever since it was established.

When studying ethnicity one cannot separate the role of ethnicity from those of social class and other variables. Middle-income Chicanos have middle-class incomes and possess some of the same values that Anglo middle-class people possess, but at the same time they are very Chicano in how they perceive and value the things and people around them. There are schools of thought in social science that state that if ethnicity (being a Chicano in the case of the Mexican American) plays a large part in people's lives, then it should be present regardless of what class they are in.

On the other side of this argument are those who think ethnicity is important only among new immigrants. Chicanos appear to be testimonials to the fact that ethnicity remains important. Many of them are not new immigrants. Their ancestors were firmly settled in the United States well before the Anglos arrived.

Ethnicity is definitely important to those who immigrated to America after the Mexican Revolution of 1910 and to those who have arrived more recently. Some social scientists have argued that the abandonment of ethnic culture is a prerequisite for upward mobility. Yet the few affluent and middle-class Hispanics of the United States have not totally given up their culture.

Donald E. Gelford (1982) contended that the two variables of class and ethnicity cannot be separated. He is correct, but the two variables also cannot be separated from other forms of achieved and ascribed status, power, prestige, and the racist-sexist ideological construct that dominates the nonminority popultion. Certainly needed are longitudinal and cross-cultural studies on not just Hispanics but also Irish, Italians, Poles, Indo-Chinese, Native Americans, Asians, and blacks.

SUMMARY

A social and cultural profile of the Chicano quickly reveals the importance of the Catholic Church for people of all ages. A variety of people—the very young, the very old, the poor, the working class, and a few professionals—all live together in barrios across the

United States. This large number of people has the extraordinary ability to cope well with one another, their economic status, tension, and their highly crowded conditions.

Although there is age stratification, the worlds of Chicano children, teenagers, young adults, adults, and seniors frequently come together. The years dividing the groups are not cemented into the social structure in a hierarchial fashion. Relationships across age groups are generally free and open. There are open, casual relationships between males and females. The unmarried as well as the married and intermarried are incorporated into the ongoing community (Blea 1980 and 1988).

Gender role prescription exists, but it sometimes becomes complicated and takes on its own unique character. Of particular interest is role casting for persons in particular circumstances, regardless of sex. For example, there is appropriate behavior for an unmarried person accompanying a married couple to a dance. The unmarried person is free to dance with the spouse, with any person of the opposite sex, with persons of all ages and status; he/she is chastised and thought badly of if he/she should get drunk, fight, use "bad language," otherwise "make a scene," or not leave at the end of the night with the people he/she came with. Rules of appropriate behavior in Chicano culture are complex and very strictly defined.

Days of observance provide a socially accepted way by which members practice cultural values. Cleanliness and a well-kept general appearance of self and home are important. Also valued are marriage, children, women, and the elderly. As the culture becomes more urbanized and internalizes more Anglo values, these Chicano values depreciate or take on other definitions and different priorities.

Chicanos aspire to copy the model American family. This desire is consistent with the American dream of a home, two cars, some children, and economic security. The substance of life—food, music, art, prayer, and relationships—are Chicano: Spanish and indigenous. The extended family, the *compadrazgo* (a form of extended family that includes godparents), the speaking of Spanish, the high regard for people and the neighborhood are of primary imprtance, as are class and race consciousness. Poverty means lack of money, but it also means not having a home or members of the community to share life with. Probably the worst thing that can happen is to not have a spouse. Life is seen as difficult, requiring a mate. Individualism is seen as Anglo, and profit is valued to the degree that it does not disrupt social relationships. Higher education and upward mobility are very good if they do not take human resources out of the barrio and alienate individuals from family.

The barrio demands people who can cope with racism and sexism. Coping skills are both negative and positive. Self-destruction, suicide, alcoholism, drug addiction, even gang activity (Moore et al. 1979) are coping mechanisms. They are alternatives. The barrio can be hard. It can be a refuge. It is psychological, physical, and social space created by discrimination and sustained by a need for survival. Gender roles are functional in an environment that is poor, crowded, laden with potential conflict, an environment where people want what American capitalism can offer but where the means to achieve it are unavailable.

REFERENCES

Blea, Irene. 1980. "Bessemer: A Sociological Perspective of a Chicano Barrio." Ph.D. diss., University of Colorado, Boulder.

———. 1988. *Bessemer*. New York: AMS Press.

Durkheim, Emile. 1915. *The Elementary Forms of the Religious Life*. London: George Allen and Unwin.

Gelford, Donald E. 1982. *Aging: The Ethnic Factor*. Boston: Little Brown.

Gilfix, Michael. 1977. "A Case of Unequal Suffering." *Generations* 3 (Summer): 8–11.

Mirande, Alfredo. 1985. *The Chicano Experience*, pp. 113–145. South Bend, IN: University of Notre Dame Press.

Moore, Joan W., Robert García, Carlos García, Luis Cerda, and Frank Valencia. 1979. *Homeboys: Gangs, Drugs and Prison in the Barrios of Los Angeles*. Philadelphia: Temple University Press.

Newquist, Deborah. 1977. "Aging Across Cultures." *Generations* 3 (Summer): 17–23.

Norwood, Robin. 1985. *Women Who Love Too Much*. New York: Simon and Schuster.

Valle, Ramón. 1977. "Natural Networks: Paths to Service." *Generations* 3 (Summer): 36–41.

4

Mexican American Female Experience

INTRODUCTION

Feminist issues came to the forefront in the mid–1960s at the height of social criticism in the United States. Some early issues were equal pay for equal work, the right of women to control their own bodies through access to birth control and abortion, and power relationships. Women wanted to be represented in higher levels of employment, education, and politics. Today the issues are not much different. Women still earn less money than men. Birth control and abortion are still issues, and women still seek to participate in higher levels of employment, education, and politics. Although some gains were made in these areas, long-term goals are far from being reached, and support organizations, advocacy groups, and pressure tactics exist as testimonials to the fact that women are far from reaching equality.

In the social sciences women have concentrated efforts on creating women's studies. They, like racial minorities, have concluded that their side of the story of the making of this nation has not been told, and they will have to tell it themselves. The studies revolved around the repression of women. Feminist scholars have designed curricula that focus upon female stereotypes; sexist language; psychological and biological gender differences; sex roles, women, and work; women and the law; the history of women; women and the capitalistic system; sexual harassment; the struggle for liberation; lesbianism; child care; violence; mothers and daughters; friends; and Third World women. Focus on Chicanas and other minority women has come under the broad topic of Third World women.

THIRD WORLD WOMEN

Concentration on Third World women was/is based upon the idea that there are two countries that control or struggle to control the world: the United States and the Soviet Union. These two countries have been referred to as two different worlds. All other countries are the Third World. This ethnocentric view places countries that are not the United States or the Soviet Union in a secondary and subordinate position. Feminists adopted the Third World label from the male-dominated society and incorporated it into their language to refer to those women who are the most disenfranchised from the dominant power structure. In the case of Chicanas, it is forgotten that they are citizens of a world power, America, and the political sisters of feminists.

Institutionalized racism created a division between minority women and other feminists. This manifested itself in the academic curriculum. Most women's studies departments and programs did not develop courses on Mexican American women and incorporate them into their curriculum until after Mexican American women developed such courses and curricula in Chicano studies. Courses on Chicanas were formulated in the 1970s. Detailed attention to Mexican American women was given in these courses. However, within the broader women's movement, minority females were barely included.

Chicana experience with American feminism is recent. White women have had a history of addressing women's issues in their society. The Chicanas' efforts to participate in this effort during the 1960s and 1970s were generally met with resistance. Chicano men initially teased and became angry. Later some joined the Chicana feminists. They laughed and called the women *comadres*. When they used this term, they used it in a demeaning, derogatory way that implied that the women had nothing better to do than "gossip" or "bitch." Those with a more critical ideological opinion said Chicana feminism was an "Anglo trip." They contended that the "Anglo trip" was not rooted in the issues of Mexican American women or the Chicano movement, but in those of middle-class white women. Men criticized women for drawing attention and energy away from

Women have been active in demonstrations resisting racist and sexist policies across the nation.

the Chicano movement and into a movement that had little to do with Chicanas. They also criticized Chicanas for destroying the basis of Chicano culture: the family. Racism, not sexism, was their concern. Chicana feminists held tight. They persisted in drawing attention to minority female concerns and noted that sexism was much like racism.

Historically those were loud, angry, hostile times. The 1960s were even violent times. Vietnam war protests, boycotts of grapes and lettuce purchases, demonstrations, and picketing were taking place. Hippies were singing love and peace songs, and wearing flowers in their hair. White youth, women, Asians, Native Americans, blacks, Chicanos, and Chicanas were active.

During this critical and crucial era Chicanos were walking out of schools to protest curricula and other unfair standards. Men and women took off traditional clothing, and strong gender-typed fashion was changed. Both men and women grew their hair long. Some females no longer shaved their underarms and legs, and free love—sex without guilt—was the order of the day. Drugs were plentiful, and poverty, simplicity, and rebelliion were common. The nation was ablaze with activity. At no other time were young adults and youth more active and visible on the streets, in schools, in the parks, everywhere. Chicanas and other minority women were few, but they effectively drew attention to their issues. At no time did they desert the Chicano movement.

Chicanas found racism abundant in the white feminist movement. They tried to tell white feminists that racism was a concern of white women because it was much like sexism, only the victims were people of color. White feminists pointed out that Mexican men were the biggest sexists of all. Chicana feminists agreed that some of them were, but that generally this stereotype of Chicano men was also racist. White feminists responded with an ultimatum: Chicanas should choose between being female and being Chicano. Chicanas could not, would not, choose. They were physically, culturally, and socially Chicano and female. Most Chicanas left the feminist movement and banded together to form the Chicana movement within the Chicano movement. They remained within the movement while asserting their feminist concerns.

In the late 1960s and the 1970s social issues were many. For Chicanas the primary issue was the cumulative effect of racism and sexism. Chicanas never criticized the Third World perspective. They understood the relationship of the powerful and the powerless in that perspective. As the white feminist movement became more sophisticated in the late 1970s, it became more concerned with involving Third World women. This, however, was mostly a concern of socialist women with strong criticism of the capitalist system. The feminist movement became fragmented because of the issues of racism, socialism, and lesbianism. Chicanas sympathized with the socialists but did not join their political party. Lesbianism was too far removed from the reality of the predominantly Catholic women. The lesbian Chicana is a relatively new concern of only a limited population.

As black and Chicano women talked and worked with one another, they discovered their experiences were much the same both in the white feminist movement and in the Chicano movement. Black women, it was discovered, were reacting much the same as Chicanos. They also remained loyal to the black civil rights movement at the same time they addressed feminist concerns. These women formed coalitions at meetings and conferences. They were among the first coalition builders among American civil rights political activists. They developed an ideology that strengthened the movement, but they remained pitted against white women and men because of racism.

FEMINIST CONFLICT IN THE CHICANO MOVEMENT

Women of color faced feminist issues with slightly different concerns. On the issues of birth control and abortion, they made extremely difficult decisions. Males of color charged that birth control was a white-planned attempt at genocide, an elimination of the ethnic group. If fewer people of color were born, whites could best control and destroy people of color. Chicanas wanted and needed control of their own bodies. They did not want men dictating what they did with their bodies. Too many children produced poverty for them, yet forced sterilization was not wanted. The practice of white doctors and other officials forcing women of color to be sterilized was a violation of female civil rights that disproportionately affected women of color. Chicanas and other women of color became expert in identifying their issues, researching them, and making necessary decisions.

In 1972, the Chicana Caucus met at the National Chicano Political Conference in San Jose, California. The conference adopted a lengthy position paper on the concerns of Chicanas and took a stand on jobs, child care, education, and abortion. At the first National Convention of La Raza Unida party in September 1972, the party pledged support of Chicana issues (Raza Unida Archives 1987). At these meetings there was resistance, but in the long run Chicanos discovered that politically sophisticated men were not as sexist as most of the nation would like to believe.

In academe there arose the National Association of Chicano Studies (NACS), which attracted 400 to 500 scholars to its annual conference in 1978. That year, NACS elected Irene I. Blea as its first female national chairperson. Hard-fought political battles sometimes are forgotten and positions of privilege are difficult to give up, but Chicano male and female activists have contributed much to changing gender roles in their culture. To some degree the grass-roots Chicanos have strayed from earlier commitments and have forgotten the earlier contributions. For these reasons it is appropriate to note that in the late 1980s the struggles persist.

A REVIEW OF CHICANA HISTORY

Dates and events documented in history are not necessarily significant to females in the same way they are to males. The Spanish conquest of Mexico, the Mexican American War, World War I, World War II, and Vietnam, as well as the influence of change in church politics, the Chicano movement, and the women's movement are significant to the Chicano people. However, the ramifications of these phenomena often have affected women differently than men because of the difference in gender roles. For example, during the Spanish conquest of Mexico, Spanish women were virtually nonexistent. Indian women, bearers of the mestizo race, were Christianized, raped, and subjected to the atrocities of slavery and war. Women's roles during the Mexican American War are not documented, but during World War I, the Great Depression, and World War II women learned to live on few resources. They raised children and worked outside the home in shipyards, on the railroads, and in ammunition factories. During the Vietnam war Chicanas protested loudly. All of these experiences and many, many more changed the sex role of women more drastically than that of men.

Chicana feminists began to publish their experiences as a body of knowledge in the late 1960s and early 1970s. Most of the writing revolved around the question of identity, and was in the form of poetry, essays, short stories, and academic articles. Mexican American women rapidly found out that they had long, proud histories of both Spanish and Indian heritage. Feminist scholars set about making the record straight by engaging in inclusionary and revisionist history. Feminists adopted aspects of the internal colonial model, the leading theoretical Chicano perspective, and focused upon the nature and character of female oppression through sexism in the society and within Chicano culture, but male-defined historical periods were adhered to.

Feminist focus proceeded to the colonial periods in both Mexico and Nueva España (New Spain), what is now the U.S. Southwest.

As Chicano studies developed, feminist scholarship developed. When men were doing Chicano labor history, the women did Chicana labor history. At the same time white women were doing white feminist studies and research. Chicanas involved themselves in these areas and focused upon male-female relationships, primarily within the family. Many women contributed to this academic movement. A review of their contributions will reveal the impact of their inclusionary activity as they documented their mestizo past.

In their monographs Flor Saiz (1973) and Martha Cotera (1976) discuss the importance of language to women. Aztec women celebrated the approaching birth of a baby with poetry. Complicated rituals were performed, and medical women would pray and attend the expectant mother. The mother would speak to the unborn child, praising it and telling it of her hopes for it. Herb teas were boiled and drunk, and upon its birth the child would be presented to the gods.

Chicana feminists combined anthropology, sociology, history, and the humanities as a means to fully capture the lives of Aztec women. These early feminist scholars focused upon the Aztecs for two reasons. The first reason is that these women had roots in the Chicano movement. The movement emphasized Aztec civilization as an example of the powerful and glorious past of the Chicano people. Another reason the Chicana feminist focused upon the Aztecs was that similar indigenous holistic medicine is still practiced by the Chicano population. Although those practicing such medicine have always included men, contemporary practitioners are primarily women. *Rezadoras* (faith healers), *sobaderas* (chiropractors), *parteras* (midwives), and *curanderas* (general practioners) utilize herbs and prayer in their healing arts.

In Southwest mental health centers *curanderas* are incorporated as part of the therapeutic staff and utilized in the treatment of psychiatric patients. One *curandera,* Diana Velázquez of Denver, has gained so much recognition that she now gives lectures and holds workshops on Chicano health and healing in foreign countries.

Chicanas have been responsible for the documentation of much of Chicano history that has been treansmitted orally from one generation to another. Some of this history has taken on legendary and mythical forms and has remained a sophisticated cultural production. One of the first women to appear in Chicano literature and oral tradition is Malintzin, around whom the legend of La Llorona has

Diana Velázquez is a powerful *curandera*. *Curanderismo* has indigenous and Spanish European origins.

been formulated and over whom there has been much controversy. Malintzin was one of 20 women given to Hernán Cortez by Montezuma when he was mistaken by the Indians for Quetzalcoatl, the light-skinned god who was to return around the time Cortez landed in Mexico in 1521. Malintzin was an intelligent, multilingual person who soon learned to speak Spanish. Cortez had the 20 women baptized and given Christian names. As Cortez traveled throughout Mexico, Malintzin, who was given the name Doña Marina, gave directions and explained the ways of the land and of the people. She was able to do this because as a child she had traveled with her parents throughout Mexico in service to the Aztec emperor, Montezuma. Her father was killed, and her mother remarried. Malintzin's mother and stepfather had a son whom they wanted to inherit their wealth. It was the Aztec tradition to grant such inheritances to the eldest child. Malintzin was sold into slavery and had passed from tribe to tribe. She learned and survived, and she came to Cortez only after another soldier discovererd her linguistic and geographic knowledge (Torres 1975). As Doña Marina she served Cortez well.

The indigenous people of Mexico, meanwhile, were calling Cortez "El Malinche" (traitor) (Díaz del Castillo 1963). As history was written in the male-dominated tradition, it recorded Doña Marina as the traitor. She has several names and appears in the literature as Malintzin, Doña Marina, La Malinche, the traitor who made it possible for Cortez to conquer Mexico.

Both Mexican and Mexican American feminists have come to the defense of La Malinche. They feel there is insufficient evidence as to whether Doña Marina performed her services voluntarily. She very well could have done what she did out of the need to survive. Rather than making the conquest the downfall of the mighty Aztec empire, she may have saved the lives of hundreds of thousands of Indians whom Cortez might have killed if she had not been involved. In addition, Cortez conquered the Aztec empire not solely with the assistance of Malintzin but also with the help of his Spanish army and many, many Mexican Indians who saw it as benefiting them or who were forced to attack the last civilization of Mexico.

When Cortez returned to Spain, he did not take Doña Marina with him. Legend says that she had a son by Cortez and that he desired to take his son to Spain. Rather than be parted from her son, Doña Marina is said to have drowned him. When she went to heaven, God would not allow her to enter until she returned with the soul of her child. The soul is said to have floated away in the river, and to this day Doña Marina, who has become La Llorona, searches the rivers and the ditches of the Southwest, crying from pain and mental anguish brought about by the never-ending search for the child's soul.

The myth has many messages for Chicanas. There is much discussion concerning the fact that Cortez never married Doña Marina in the church and that he used her to satisfy sexual impulses and the needs of the expedition. Many believe that God was angry with Doña Marina for having engaged in this affair and for having conceived an illegitimate child. Little attention is given to the fact that Cortez was a willing party with more power and influence. Nevertheless, the message warns women against illegitimate children, premarital sex, and deviation from the nurturing, mother role. The consequences are overwhelming and never ending. The story also exemplifies the oppressive influence of the church and its doctrine. Extreme social pressure is exerted on women to stay well within their sex role. Doña Marina did not passively accept Cortez's decision to take their son and was punished for it.

In traditional culture, males have believed they receive certain privileges because they are males, and one of those privileges is to not be questioned or confronted by women on any issue. The Chicana movement strove to overcome such conditions, but also to sustain rich Chicano culture. The problem, however, was that the culture sometimes was consistent with female oppression.

Continuing with the legend of La Llorona will lend some insight. Some people say she will steal any child, kill it, and take its soul in an attempt to fool God and gain entrance to heaven.

This version of the story tends to depict women as evil, cruel, cheating, and in general immoral and unethical. Men are also made to appear dishonest, disloyal, and sexually promiscuous, but the way the story is told implies that it is the woman's fault. The legend presents very negative views of males and females; but it does keep children away from dangerous rivers and irrigation ditches where they might drown, and it does get them home before dark.

It is sometimes reported that La Llorona is on the telephone. It appears that in the early 1980s Austin, Texas, teenagers engaging in long telephone conversations with their friends would be interrupted by loud crying and scary noises. Parents would tell the teens to hang up or La Llorona would get them. When my scholarly friend shared this news with me, I became aware that La Llorona is the oldest living female influence in the Americas. She has endured from Meso-American pre-Columbian times to contemporary high-technological society. Nowhere else has a figure female had this experience.

La Llorona serves as a symbol to the women of the Spanish-language world. She has dignity, value, and worth. She is strong, human, and loving. She loves deeply and pragmatically. Insight into the Indian culture of the time reveals that Malintzin did not want Cortez to take the child to Spain because she knew the Spanish were different from the Indians, that Spain was a strange place, that her son would surely die on the long voyage if not because of the strangeness of a different land. Malintzin believed that if her son died away from his own land, his spirit would never rest. She killed her child to save his spirit from an indigenously prescribed eternal damnation, one she endured at the hands of the Spanish.

The conquest of Mexico significantly changed the lives of Indian women. It also introduced Spanish women to the New World, which was really an old world, and led to new ways of living. Indian women once reigned as goddesses, but after the conquest they wore the facial brands of slavery and were subjected to the imposition of a male Christian God. Three centuries of European colonialism demanded forced labor. Women worked in the mines. They provide domestic and sexual services, and the tallow for candles used in the rich ore and mineral mines. They worked in the silk industry, sugar mills, chocolate mills, and wineries. They were bakers and held many other positions in the economy of the time. The conquest brought another powerful woman: the Virgin Mary, the Virgin of Guadalupe, the Catholic patron saint of Mexico.

The Indians suffered cultural destruction during Mexico's colonial period, but some of that culture was integrated into the Spanish culture. Gods and goddesses of the earth, the underworld, and the heavens were replaced with concepts symbolized by Jesus and Mary and the devil. The Catholic friars are reported to have baptized, confirmed, and married most if not all of Mexico by 1572. Today, Chicana feminists point to the church as one of the most oppressive institutions. The church is charged with exerting influence that did not allow women to define their own lives. Feminists also view the church as resisting change and as oppressive in not recognizing the dissolution of marriages, taking a firm stance against birth control and abortion, and not allowing women to be priests.

CHICANAS NORTH OF MEXICO

The first recorded European to go north of Mexico into the Southwest was Avaro Nuñez Cabeza de Vaca in 1528. From his experience as prisoner of an Indian tribe we get some insight into the role of Southwest Indian women. Cabeza de Vaca reported having been treated as a squaw. He described his work as woman's work and reported that he dug for roots, gathered firewood, built fires, fished, and learned the healing arts. History reports that the priests taught the Indians much, but little is mentioned concerning what the Indians taught the priests. The Indians taught the white man how to do the things that Cabeza de Vaca reports he did. This was worthwhile and necessary work, work done by women.

Hundreds of Spanish-speaking and Indian women have gone unrecognized and unmentioned for their contributions in the settlement of the Southwest. Feminist writers cite Francisca de Hozas as one such woman. She is referred to as "... an outspoken wench who kept her husband on a leash and controlled him" (Saiz 1973). Flor Saiz notes that if the situation were reversed, the husband would be praised for keeping his wife "in her place." Francisca de Hozas is reported to have made her contribution by offering ideas concerning the direction of Coronado's expedition. Her direction was taken reluctantly but proved to be in the best interests of all. She began the expedition with an eight-year-old child and gave birth to a second child before it was over. Other women in the Coronado expedition were Maria Maldonado and Señora Caballero. Maldonado was an older woman who nursed the ill and mended their clothing. Caballero was also an older woman. Her Indian background enabled her to relate stories and information about the territory, its climate, and its people.

In 1540 a large group of women—wives and daughters of Spanish soldiers and Indian men—traveled with Coronado on yet another expedition. These women cared for the ill, repaired torn and worn clothing, cooked, and cared for infants as well as men. All this was done while traveling on horseback or walking, living out of wagons, and being subjected to heat, cold, wild animals, and Indians who were sometimes hostile. The description of early Spanish and Indian women who were the Chicanas' ancestors reads much like those of the early pioneer Anglo women, who did not arrive until three centuries later. By the time white women arrived, Spanish-speaking women had experienced and mastered most of what concerned them on the frontier, but there is no evidence that they interrelated.

Meanwhile, Mexico was experiencing its colonial period. One of the greatest literary figures of the world, Sor Juana Inez de la Cruz, was the first woman in the Americas to openly question male domination. She was born a Creole in 1648, and was placed in school at the age of three. De la Cruz advanced far beyond the nuns' expectations, and by the age of eight was writing plays and poetry. From her physically comfortable but socially conflicted life we learn that women were not allowed to pursue advanced study. Her mother cut de la Cruz's hair and allowed her to dress in boy's clothing so she could continue her studies. De la Cruz incorporated into her writings various areas of knowledge and science. She symbolizes to Chicanas a highly sophisticated intellectual feminist. Among her writings are *Las Redondillas,* a collection of poems dealing with male-female issues, and *Contra las Injusticias de Hombre al Hablar de la Mujer* ("Against the Injustices of Men in Talking About Women").

There are many more women who deserve mention and about whom relatively little has been written in Mexico and, especially, in the United States. Among those women are the social activists Sor Felipe de Jesús, Sor Antonia Perez de los Santos, Sor Rosa, Sor Antonio de la Santísima Trinidad, and Rosa de Loreto, all of whom were Indian women who attended the Convento de Corpus Christi.

Also worthy of investigation is Gertrudis Bocanegra, who organized an effort for Indians' education. The government felt that her actions were unfeminine and that they threatened the government, because if Indians learned to read and write, they might revolt. Bocanegra was active in 1810, the year of the Grito de Dolores (the cry for independence). She organized small underground armies of women who smuggled supplies to the battlefield. She was taken prisoner, questioned, and tortured. On October 17, 1817, she was executed for not cooperating with supporters of the status quo. Like many other women, her activities and contributions went unrecognized (in her case, for 120 years). Other women involved in the early Mexican revolutions include Josefa Ortiz de Domínguez, "La Correjadora," Leona Vicario, Juana Bebn Gutiérrez de Mendoza, Señora Flores de Andrada, Dolores Jiménez y Muro, and Guadalupe Rojo de Alvarado. These women were instrumental in establishing revolutionary magazines and newspapers, and feminist organizations, and in fighting on the battlefields. They serve as role models for Chicana feminists.

The Mexican Revolution of 1910 brought additional role models and changes to the women of Mexico. Chicana feminist scholars have incorporated the social revolution into their scholarship. During the Mexican Revolution families were disrupted and women were forced to march with the men. Children were born without fathers present. Fathers and husbands were killed, and so were women. On the more positive side, women came into contact with new geographical locations and learned more about the land and its people. Most important of all, women learned about politics, and after the war they utilized that knowledge to better not only their personal living conditions but also the conditions of others. Divorce laws were liberalized, some maternity leave for employed women was established, and so were laws regulating employment and dangerous occupations. All this was done before these issues were addressed in the United States. Another revolutionary change came in the attempt to eliminate the stigma of illegitimacy and prostitution. For the American Chicana, La Adelita, the female soldier, became a revolutionary role model in the 1960s and 1970s.

As the American West developed, Chicanos became increasingly displaced from the land, especially after 1848 and the end of the Mexican-American War. Francisca Reyes Esparza arose to address the issue of displacement from the land. While attempting to gather evidence to file a land-grant lawsuit for title to 250,000 acres of oil and ranch land, she was successful in developing communictions between the United States and Mexico. She became an expert on the historical aspects of land titles guaranteed to Mexican-American citizens under Article VIII of the Treaty of Guadalupe Hidalgo. In 1946, she won her case and set in motion vehicles that are utilized today on those same issues. Esparza's contributions are overshadowed by those of Burt Corona, praised by today's Chicano leaders and academics for the labor causes he pursued.

Another Chicana overshadowed by Corona is Josefina Fierro, who became active during the mass deportations of the 1930s. She was active in bringing back Mexican-American citizens from Mexico. In the early 1940s she joined Corona in organizing low-paid Hispanic workers in canneries and on farms. Fierro was also instrumental in ending the violent racist and sexist conflicts between Chicano citizens and U.S. servicemen after World War II in Los Angeles. By negotiating with Vice-President Wallace to declare Los Angeles out of bounds to military personnel, she became the most important person in the termination of the "zoot suit" conflicts. Many Chicano history books make these "zoot riots" appear to be solely racist in nature, but the truth is that they were also sexist. Chicanas were the victims of U.S. servicemen, who considered them to be cheap prostitutes and/or infected with venereal disease and addicted to marijuana. Women were being slandered and harassed by American servicemen. Interviews with ex-"zoot suiters" reveal that Chicanos were also sexist in their attitudes toward Chicanas. The Hispanic men felt the women were their women, and did not want to share them with the gringo. Much fighting took place. Today the Chicana still suffers from such racist/sexist stereotypes.

This text would not be completed without mention of Chicana activists in the labor market. Emma Tenayuca and Dolores Huerta are but two of a large group of women that includes Lucy Parsons, Luisa Moreno, and many faceless and nameless individuals. Tenayuca is best remembered for her participation in the San Antonio, Texas, pecan shellers' strike in 1938. She was the principal organizer and spokesperson representing primarily Chicana workers. Workers were protesting wages and work conditions. The strike was extremely successful but lost significance when the processing plants were mechanized and the workers displaced. Worker displacement is still a labor issue, and Tenayuca still engages in dialogue on such issues. Struggle against oppressive forces has been a life-style for many Chicanas.

A contemporary issue in which Chicanas are, and always have been, involved is farm workers' conditions. Dolores Huerta's contributions have been overshadowed by media coverage of César Chávez. Equal in involvement and commitment in the struggle to organize a union and promote negotiations with corporate farmers, Huerta worked side by side with Chávez and others in the boycotts, demonstrations, picketings, and sit-ins. Huerta organized many of these activities, and she lobbied for changes in child welfare, health, and education, She extended those efforts to include all migrants, and withstood criticism and physical abuse at the hands of those resistant to her efforts. Dolores Huerta certainly rates mention in America's labor history.

Many women have organized to resist domination. They have been instrumental in protecting workers' rights and have organized in the fields, factories, communities, and industrial plants across the land. Many of these women have taken part in major efforts, such as the Farah Slack strike and boycott that began on May 9, 1972. During this effort 4000 Chicano workers, mostly women, walked off their jobs.

Feminist Chicanas have marched and protested the killing of their people by police, and they have criticized sexist and racist education, repressive religion, and rape and other attacks on women. These women have a history of creativity. They continue to struggle and create against oppressive forces both in their own culture and in the general society. This creativity is extended into the social sciences, where Chicana feminist scholars have merged to examine earlier work. Early feminists are not offended by this examination. They are well aware that they are engaged in a battle of ideas, and that ideas have to be able to withstand criticism or change. At the forefront of early feminist scholarship were Marcella Trujillo, Inez Hernández-Tovar, Martha Cotera, Inez Talamantez, Lea Yberra, Maxine Baca-Zinn, Anna Nieto Gómez, and Irene I. Blea.

SOCIAL STRATIFICATION IN ACADEME

The battle of ideas is over how people think. This affects how they behave. Chicano feminists brought their ideas to campuses across the United States, but in higher education the setting reinforces inequality. As Chris Sierra (Cordova et al. 1986) has so aptly stressed, the power of academe rests upon ideas. It is hierarchical and selective. The myth is that university and college campuses have been places that foster free thinking. At a theoretical level this is true. However, the campus is characterized by human politics, and much power is exerted to control who teaches on campus and what is taught. Women's studies and Chicano studies have been opposed by faculty in traditional disciplines, and racism and sexism have been used to keep Chicanos and women off campus and out of classes. Campus struggles for power and prestige are vicious, and the stratified system found in the general society is dominant. Nevertheless, Chicanos and Chicanas have managed to keep the curriculum alive.

The Chicanas' major contribution has been a theoretical perspective on race, class, and sex. They have combined their experience to form a multifaceted analysis that does not separate these factors. Women's studies has tended to focus on the female experience at the expense of race and class. This has worked against the study of the Chicana. Womanhood has been not a universal experience, but one that is class- and race/ethnic-relevant (Baca-Zinn et al. 1986). The Chicanas' theoretical discussions on discrimination have been influenced by Karl Marx's analysis, the civil rights scholars of race relations, and feminism. In researching and writing about minority females, it is necessary to view racism and sexism as related kinds of discrimination with shared characteristics. In an analysis somewhat like Karl Marx's class analysis, yet different from it, differential treatment is based on biological and ascribed social criteria.

In 1972, Shulamith Firestone, in *The Dialectic of Sex,* pointed out that sexism was so ingrained into American society that it was invisible. Subsequent feminist discussions focused upon the history of feminism and the social-psychological mechanisms of discrimination based on sex. Feminist literature, as well as literature on ethnic and racial minorities, has established that discrimination is a historical experience. Feminist literature, along with Chicano and black literature, has upheld the notion that discrimination is an ever-constant, ever-changing social control phenomenon that keeps pace with historical times and exists because it functions to support American values of competition, profit, and domination. Racism and sexism have been historically effective mechanisms by which the ruling elite has controlled resources, status, power, and prestige. A model of the historical progression of discrimination can be made clearer when the experience of minority women is analyzed.

What is important in the discussion of women of color is not race or sex or class, but discrimination as experienced sometimes based on race, sometimes based on sex, sometimes based on class, and sometimes based on all three. This makes the analysis complex and sometimes confusing. This confusion is not necessary if one takes the perspective that the discriminatory process is virtually the same in all these cases. The victim changes.

Victimization can be better understood if the dominant Western thought process is very briefly reviewed. It is a hierarchical one consisting of binary opposition ranging from "low in value" to "high in value." There is a tendency to think in categories exemplified by good-bad, in-out, black-white, up-down, male-female. If individuals are in categories that have less value or worth (less money, less education, less political power), they are ascribed a negative value with little or no access to power, status, privilege, or prestige.

In the colored-noncolored dichotomy, persons of color become locked into a social cycle of poverty much like the one Gunnar Myrdal presented in 1944. The same happens to the lesser-valued female in the male-female dichotomy. The study of the economics of the black experience expanded Myrdal's notion and demonstrated how the factors of the cycle of poverty were even more controlling than Myrdal had supposed. The effect of discrimination on education, for example, did more than establish a cycle of low employment, low political power, and low health standards. The cycle could also be reversed: low health standards lead to low political power, low employment, and low education.

In addition, each variable can affect the variable opposite it in the cycle. The result is a multifaceted, social-psychological phenomenon that depresses the victim's social experience. A better approach to the vicious cycle of poverty should include a discussion of how the cementing of the cycle of discrimination is multifaceted.

If women are placed in the center of the cycle as scapegoats of discrimination, it can be observed that the process is the same as if minorities are at the center. If minority women are at the center of the cycle, the double discrimination affecting them becomes ever clearer: The stress of opposing forces is doubled. These women definitely are cemented into the cycle of discrimination.

Discrimination does not begin in any of the variables as practiced. It begins at the cognitive level. In the tradition of Frantz Fanon (1963) and Albert Memmi (1965), members of the dominant group believe they are the most worthy and define their own worthiness. They institute psychological and social mechanisms by which to convince the oppressed of the worthiness of the dominant group. When the oppressed internalize this idea, the dominant group is believed to be the most worthy. The subordinate group struggles against being like the dominant group's image of itself. The cycle of discrimination at the cognitive level is complete when the dominant group places barriers to social acceptance of the subordinate group in the dominant group's minds. The function of keeping the minority group in an adverse power relationship is the role of discrimination. The behavioral discrimination cycle is complete when the subordinate group is unble to prove that the image the dominant group has of it is not true. This process begins at the level of thinking or having an idea. It gives itself shape and development through action and a series of discriminating behaviors.

Mario Barrera (1979) has documented that racial prejudice in the work place increases competition between Anglo workers and racial-ethnic minority workers. At the same time that racism increases production via competition, it lessens the recognition that owners

Multifaceted Cycle of Discrimination

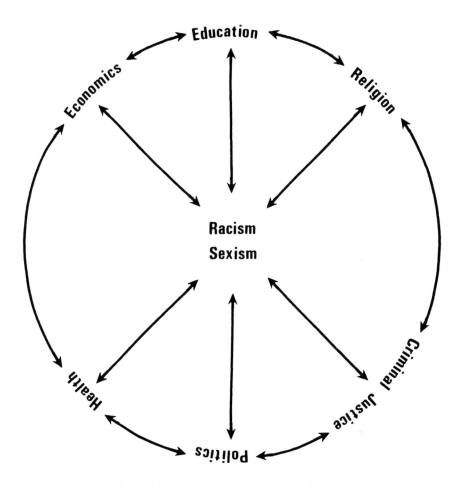

of the means of production are exploiting both Chicano and Anglo worker populations.

This observation, and the multifaceted nature of the discrimination cycle, can be applied to male-female relations. If men and women believe and live out prescribed sex roles on the job, female wages and working conditions will remain low, and male wages and conditions will not improve. Generally, men will accept the status quo with the rationalization that their wages and conditions are at least better than women's. Thus, males not only support female oppression but also contribute to their own oppression by invisible social controlling forces whose objective is not to pay male or female workers the worth of their production.

If Chicanos and Chicanas believe in prescribed sex roles, they enter into prescribed gender role relationships. Such personal relationships are set up for antagonism because it is assumed that each individual and his/her partner are not going to change attitude or behavior. If the partners stay within a limited definition, they may be able to maintain the relationship, but if either of them changes or questions the situation, conflict is sure to follow. As long as partners remain in prescribed sex role relationships, the true oppressor, the system that upholds male-female discrimination, cannot be recognized as exploiting the male and oppressing female talent and opportunity. To deviate from a prescribed sex role is not to allow exploitation and oppression to occur, at least through the social-psychological process of internalization. The same is true of racism and classism: to deviate from a prescribed race-class role is not to allow racism and discrimination based on class to continue unquestioned.

CONTEMPORARY CHICANA FEMINIST ISSUES

Counteracting classism, racism, and sexism requires considerable thought and complicated action. Working with and teaching minority women has revealed a cycle that has not yet been encountered in the literature. Not much research has been conducted upon persons who have escaped or who have successfully managed the multifceted dimensions of discrimination. It is known that individuals trapped by triple discrimination find themselves in conditions of unhappiness, poverty, and immobility. They have to think and act in ways that permit them to subsist and to escape the negative social consequences of stepping out of a prescribed social role. Through a process of creative trial and error, some arrive at behaviors that more or less work for them.

Much of the literature by minority women about minority women is still trying to counteract stereotypes and negative images. It is true that some minority women suffer degrees of alienation, powerlessness, and bad self-images, but most of them live and create in this unfavorable environment. They have periods of highs and lows, but they also have extensive periods of equilibrium and high productivity. When they are functioning at as highly motivated level, they are overachievers, personable, and extremely powerful. Perhaps their outstanding quality is flexibility and lateral thinking. Because they have had to overcome significant barriers, they have learned to address issues, to attack problems in ways that are entirely new to those who have not had their experience.

Because of their unique experiences, women of color are on the verge of developing a new paradigm in the social sciences. Social reality is composed of multifaceted phenomena that are specific to populations and individuals. This perspective does not negate social scientific thinking. It incorporates it and lends a new perspective while allowing for the inclusion of experiences that prior to this were exceptions to established social theory. Women and racial-ethnic minorities have frequently been the exception. This new perspective accounts for the unique experience of women and racial-ethnic minorities, yet includes the experiences of others.

Keep in mind that the Chicana's contribution is not rooted only in her oppression. It is also rooted in her creative, sustaining experience. For example, the Chicana of the contemporary Chicano movement is able to communicate across race, class, and gender. She is able to function in higher education as well as interact with the poorest, most illiterate in the barrio. She can organize a fund raiser, write an article, and get it all done at the same time. This woman is often called "super Chicana" because she is a Renaissance woman. She is also politically sophisticated in the workings of racism, classism, and sexism. She understands the social system, what keeps it from changing, and what causes it to change.

A discussion of a new model of discrimination must turn to oppression by the oppressed. Internalized racism, classism, and sexism manifest themselves among and between members of discriminated-against groups. Sexism and racism are exerted upon women and men of noncolor by women and men of color. Not only is sexism exercised against women by men, it is also a female-to-female and male-to-male endeavor.

It is easy to recognize male sexism as it manifests against females, and it can be just as easy to recognize sexism directed at men. Women, including minority women, have certain expectations of men. They believe men should be successful according to a dominant definition of what is successful. When men cannot live up to female expectations, they lose value in the female opinion. The hardest sexist blows are received by minority men. Minority men are also victims of the "double whammy." The successful role model for men is white, tall and strong, economically secure, and healthy, with status, power, and prestige. The minority male is at an extreme disadvantage. It is impossible for him to be an American male social success when the vehicles for success are not accessible. Minority females are recognizing this fact and need to stop placing pressure on their men to meet the noncolored dominant male's criteria for success.

SUMMARY

To discriminate means to choose one thing over another. In society it has come to mean exclusion and exploitation of a group or person. There are at least three basic premises for discrimination: psychological, biological, and social. The consequences of discrimination are felt in these areas.

In the discriminating society, dark skin color has come to mean "lesser in value." Women have been considered less in value. This degradation begins with stereotypes. Race or skin color, like gender, is a natural biological condition, but it triggers certain negative images and responses. A woman of color triggers off a double response, one based on sex and one based on race. Because most people believe women of color are poor, it is reasonable to expect that the discrimination will quickly move into a set of stereotypes about poor people.

These responses are so closely related that it is difficult to decipher which comes first. Rather than deal with this confusion, the racist-sexist-classist does not attempt communication of any kind. Differential treatment of minority women stimulates certain areas of the brain and body, but it also places extreme pressure upon women to internalize social messages that are disadvantageous to them. Most minority female workers are overworked and underpaid. These facts may set up conditions for low self-esteem, low self-concept, and behavior that appears unmotivated. The minority woman, however, does not always live in such a depressed psychological state. She has developed her own coping mechanisms and has the potential to develop new paradigms.

William Ryan stated that populations that are discriminated against are targets of aggression, avoidance, and neglect (1971). They appear not to live up to the criteria of the dominant society. The Chicana exceeds all expectations and is an overachiever.

REFERENCES

Baca-Zinn, Maxine, Lynn Cannon, Elizabeth Higgenbotham, and Bonnie Thorton Dill. 1986. "The Costs of Exclusionary Practices in Women's Studies." *Signs: Journal of Women in Culture and Society* 2, no. 21: 290–303.

Barrera, Mario. 1979. *Race and Class in the Southwest.* South Bend, IN: University of Notre Dame Press.

Cordova, Theresa, Norma Cantu, Gilberto Cardenas, Juan García, and Christine M. Sierra. 1986. *Chicana Voices: Intersections of Class, Race and Gender.* Austin: University of Texas, CMAS Publications.

Cotera, Martha. 1976. *Diosa y Hembra.* Austin, TX: Information Systems Development.

Díaz del Castillo, Bernal. 1963. *The Conquest of New Spain.* New York: Penguin Books.

Fanon, Frantz. 1963. *The Wretched of the Earth.* New York: Grove Press.

Firestone, Shulamith. 1972. *The Dialectic of Sex.* New York: Bantam Books.

Memmi, Albert. 1965. *The Colonizer and the Colonized.* Boston: Beacon Press.

Myrdal, Gunnar. 1944. *An American Dilemma.* New York: Harper.

Raza Unida Archives. 1987. Conference report. Austin: University of Texas. Benson Latin American Collection.

Ryan, William. 1971. *Blaming the Victim.* New York: Vintage Books.

Saiz, Flor. 1973. *La Chicana.* Denver: La Chicana Publications.

Torres, J. Jesús Figueroa. 1975. *Doña Marina: Una India Ejemplar.* Mexico City: B. Costa-AMIC Editor.

5
Social Control and the Chicano Experience

INTRODUCTION

Everything in society has a reason for existing. A Mexican game or a Mexican American dance is a wonderful experience in collective behavior. It is behavior in which those present are swept away, incorporated into the excitement of what is happening. It happens often without effort. American concerts and football games sometimes provide the same experience, but the sense of intimacy is usually missing. These activities generally function to allow people to express many emotions in a way that is not threatening to the society. Music, games, art, poetry, and sports reach into the human experience and exhibit the soul or the core of what composes it. These activities are an integral part of Chicano life because involved in these activities are certain rules. But the Chicano also has to learn other rules: Anglo rules that are written and unwritten.

Chicano dances gather crowds. People frequently pay to get into dances, and many have earned their living by running nightclubs and playing music for dancing. These crowds generate a tremendous cohesiveness, a consensus. There is power where there is a Chicano dance because there is mutual understanding of things that are very intimate.

CHICANO SOCIETY

In most Chicano gatherings one will find a sense of camaraderie. At a Chicano dance several things are happening. Chicano society is being exposed. There are norms and values on exhibit. The best dances are those that are nonroutine. The wedding or *quincinera* dance is an excellent example. Individuals are invited, but an unstated invitation is also extended to family and friends. Thus, Chicanos feel free to bring others with them to a reception and dance. This makes Chicano weddings very large.

Chicano dances bring together a very special kind of group. Unlike traditional American groups, it does not have common status, power, and prestige. The group generally is composed of Chicanos from various income levels, ages, and mental and physical abilities. There is little homogeneity to the group outside of the fact that they are Chicano and they have come to a wedding reception and dance. Good things happen at weddings. Old friends and family members reunite. Food and drink are shared. Many smiles and hugs are exchanged. People receive acknowledgment. They fit positively or negatively, but they fit. One does not go to a wedding dance as a stranger. People assume they know one another, if for no other reason than that they are sharing the experience. This is unlike similar Anglo functions, where the idea of fitting in is important and where a place is attached to the idea of fitting in.

Very few studies have been done on Chicano group behavior. Most of what has been done has been assessed deviant. Most attention to Chicano group behavior has gone to gangs and the Chicano movement, and frequently feeds racist academic tendencies and stereotypes. There is a need for studies focusing on what supports Chicano culture. The Chicano as creator and sustainer should be focused upon in order to create balance.

SOCIAL DEVIANCE AND THE CHICANO COMMUNITY

Statistical social deviance is measured in the degree to which individuals deviates from those who conform to the norm. For Chicanos there are two norms: an Anglo norm and a Chicano norm. Frequently the norms are the same, but not always and not always in the same way. Chicanos stray from cultural prescriptions for a

Quincineras present young women to their communities. Those parents who can afford them host large coming-out parties on their daughter's fifteenth birthday.

variety of reasons, but the most frequent reason is to engage in interaction with the Anglo culture. Just as the Anglo sees Chicano culture as different or even deviant, so the Chicano views Anglo culture as different and deviant. The degree to which it is defined as deviant depends on what kind of violations take place. One kind of behavior may seem eccentric in one situation but at another time or place may be deviant. Generally both cultures recognize deviance when strong cultural norms are violated. Thus, few acts are intrinsically deviant, and deviance is relevant to cultural norms—it often changes from culture to culture.

Generally the powerful impose definitions of what is deviant upon the less powerful. Often, a definition of deviance is placed on the behavior of the less powerful that is very normal for the powerful. This is called a double standard. For instance, sociologists have noted that most Americans drive over 55 miles an hour when the speed limit is 55, that the majority of young Americans smoke marijuana, and that a high number drink and drive.

Usually the study of deviance has two concerns. One focus is upon who is doing the defining; the other is upon who is being defined. Agents of the powerful group, the police or government officials, define and enforce punishment against deviant acts and the people who engage in them. Governing bodies and those implementing policy concern themselves with who breaks the rules at a formal level, and there are informal rules that also are monitored.

There exist unspoken rules in the society. One can visualize a cultural norm as a rule establishing what is culturally acceptable. What is culturally acceptable is a guideline, an area of palatable behavior. Outside this arena, social behavior becomes distasteful, hardly tolerable, and even unacceptable. The more a person or group deviates from the norm, the less the behavior is valued. There are statistical models that reflect standard deviations from the norm, which means the degree to which people or groups deviate from what is defined as normal. Generally, the further one deviates from the norm, the smaller the number of people represented and the higher the deviance.

Sociologists focus attention in three areas. Perhaps the most frequently cited explanation for what causes deviance is Emile Durkheim's (1966) concept of anomie. As society grows and changes, the norms become more unclear and people are more diverse. The old norms are no longer applicable, and because people need norms, they

Distribution of Social Behavior

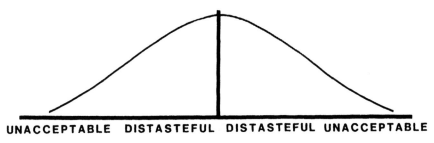

UNACCEPTABLE   DISTASTEFUL   DISTASTEFUL   UNACCEPTABLE

HARDLY TOLERABLE   NORMAL   HARDLY TOLERABLE

commit suicide. Robert Merton (1957) made an outstanding contribution to the field when he asserted that some individuals do not find the norms relevant to them, thus increasing their potential for deviance. This model stopped focusing on the individual to pay attention to the social structure and how that structure bans some individuals from attaining the means by which they can be "normal." Such is the Chicano condition. Given most American values and norms, the Chicanos cannot be normal in American society. The social system will not allow Chicanos near the Anglo standard— materially, physically, or emotionally. Thus, it is normal for Chicanos to be abnormal within the context of white dominant American society, because much of it is dictated by Anglos.

Chicano resistance threatens Anglo dominance, so Anglo society places pressure on Chicanos to be like Anglos. The Hispanic population is large—soon it will be the largest ethnic population in the United States. Rational people are having a difficult time understanding why in a democracy such a large population is a "minority." White America does not want this question asked. Nor does it want its people to know that people of color are set up to be anomic deviants. The dominant society sets minorities up to accept or strive to meet the white majority's goals but blocks them from achieving those goals.

Another theory frequently used to understand deviance is the cultural transmission theory. Most representative of this perspective is Edwin Sutherland's (1961) differential association theory, which assumes that deviance is learned through interaction with others. In cultural transmission theories, deviant norms and values are "passed on" or transmitted as cultural characteristics in neighborhoods. This "blame the victim" perspective is as dangerous to Chicanos as is the "culture of poverty" model. Sutherland's work is especially harmful because it has set the tone of research and theory since its appearance. It fails to recognize the social factors that contribute to a definition of deviance that victimizes people of color.

Some social-control theorists (Hirschi 1969; Krohn and Massey 1980; Nye 1958; Reckless 1973; Wiatrowski et al. 1981) see deviance as a natural condition, and it is its absence that needs focus. Hirschi (1969) suggests that deviance is absent when people are strongly bonded to society. When people are strongly bonded, society is exerting powerful, informal social control. When they are weakly bonded, informal control is weak.

Chicano scholars (Mirande 1985; Barrera 1979) have documented that there are both formal and informal standards placed upon the Chicano. At the formal (manifest) level, Chicanos are equal under the law. At the informal level there are special rules that apply to people of color. The double standard and how it functions are not recognized by many, but it does produce weak social bonding to the dominant norm. Some Chicanos cannot trust most Anglos. Anglo deviance is normal to those Chicanos. Many Chicanos are persons of their word. They traditionally have been cooperative. Because Chicanos have not accepted all Anglo norms and values, and because they have their own norms and values, they are not as strongly controlled in the informal way that Anglos are controlled by their own society. The Chicanos, of course, have endured negative social consequences for resisting.

The Chicano is very much aware that there are a double standard of behavior, a dual wage system, dual criminal justice standards, and dual opportunities. They see this double standard of justice, education, and judgment of cultural productions such as literature and art. They have seen and felt the negative attitudes directed at them when they note that there are more blacks and Chicanos in the criminal justice system as cases and as prisoners, and that few Chicanos are representatives of that system. They know police officers have killed and brutally beaten Chicano men, women, and children.

When America boasts about its peaceful nature, the myth of peaceful progress, Chicanos grin, raise an eyebrow, and recognize the lies and distortions. They recognize distortions in Anglo media. For example, the American media use the peaceful nature of Chicanos against them. In the not-too-distant past, Mexican Americans were called the "sleeping giant" or the "awakening minority." The peaceful element of Chicano culture was linked to words that implied largeness but dumbness, ignorance, and laziness. Whether or not this was the intention is irrelevant. Americans and the way they use their language could not help but conjure up images that were and still are detrimental. At no time have the media examined—in schools, colleges, universities, textbooks, TV, radio, newspapers, or magazines—the peaceful nature of social-cultural and political resistance such as exhibited in the Penitente tradition, language retention, and the use of music and art.

Chicanos have created an ideology that believes in a higher being, an ideology that has Christian and Indian spiritual components. Chicanos value music and art, being able to speak two languages, and surviving with family and friends. They value their Chicanismo, their Mexicanness, and their Americanness. That is why they celebrate the Fourth of July, the Cinco de Mayo, and the Sixteenth of September. These holidays celebrate freedom. They are patriotic holidays. Chicanos value political participation. The Cinco de Mayo and the Dieciseis de Septiembre, as well as the Mexican Revolution, have made them political participants. Chicanos value themselves; they love their people.

This is what dominant America is afraid of: people who take part in life, people who live it, people who love it, appreciate it, and want to give it direction. Chicanos are people with strong character. Dominant white America fears strong people who demand social, cultural, and political participation. America fears those who criticize, those who truly believe in democracy and equality. America fears those who want to see its promises realized. It fears those who seek the truth and live their lives honestly, demanding honesty and dignity from others. America fears the Chicanos will speak to the world. That is why it seeks to silence them by keeping them from succeeding in education, from writing or speaking well in two languages. This is why it seeks to segregate the population, to keep it poor, to whip it when it tries to leave its social-psychological space. It expects Chicanos to live "down" to one expectation and Anglos to live "up" to another. Ruthlessly, Anglo society exerts pressure on the community to produce well below the Anglo norm.

COLLECTIVE BEHAVIOR AND A MODEL OF RESISTANCE

The American media have given some attention to Chicanos attempting to change the social system that oppresses them. In the

Mexican independence celebrations are a festive time for all.

1960s they showed crowd shots of Chicanos with fists thrust in the air as they yelled "Chicano, Chicano, Chicano Power!" Most nonminority Americans formulated their first impressions of Chicanos through the media and have not changed their outlook. They think of Chicanos as being angry, as "acting out," as demanding, as un-American, and as frightening. Nonminority America has not realized that the Chicano movement began in the 1960s and that the population has changed. Racism and sexism are still with us, and every once in a while the minority population must organize to remind dominant America that they are still victims of exclusion and discrimination. White America sees these reminders as threatening collective actions.

Collective actions, in the minds of most Americans, involve episodic behavior by groups of people. These behaviors are motivated by nonroutine events and include mob actions and riots. In contrast, the Chicano civil rights movement was deliberately organized for the purpose of implementing social change. The desired change was at the institutional level, which would affect the norms and values of the social fabric. Usually this change is exerted from outside, but with the Chicano movement there were attempts at change from inside the system. Advocates of change included educators, politicians, health providers, social workers, and media reporters. A social movement hardly ever occurs when there is viable participation in society. It is when participation is denied that the need for a social movement is warranted.

There are two forms of social movements: reform and revolutionary. The Chicano movement consisted of both elements. A reformist movement sought change without severely altering the social structure. This kind of movement wanted to participate in the ongoing structure. The revolutionary movement sought to alter the social structure: to change it entirely, to build a new society.

Most Americans have not studied social movements and are unfamiliar with social movement theory. On their radios and TVs and in their newspapers they saw mobs of people, angry and demanding. Those mobs appeared to have little organization, and most Americans were shocked and critical of the Chicano movement. Some Chicanos also were critical of it. The criticisms that the Chicano movement endured were made because Chicanos had to go outside legitimate channels to address their issues. Much like the social bandit, the Chicano movement became labeled deviant and unnecessary by the dominant culture. It was during this time that Chicano scholars developed their own model for understanding their social-historical experience in the United States. The internal colonial model is still the dominant model in Chicano studies.

Chicano scholar Mario Barrera (1979) stated that internal colonialism involves a historical relationship of ethnic/racial subordination that coincides with regional population concentration. An essential feature of the model is a situation in which an outside group dominates and exploits a group indigenous to the land through systematic discrimination. Carlos Muñoz (1972) maintained that dominant-minority relations are characterized by racism and that the cultural minority comprises a "third world" within the boundaries of the United States. In Chicano studies there has emerged a school of thought that is consistent with the writings of Barrera and Muñoz. Within the internal colonial model Chicanos are presented as having entered a relationship with the Anglos on an involuntary basis. This relationship is characterized by violent conflict and has been maintained through Anglo force. A crucial distinguishing factor is the legal status of the colonized. The colony is internal if the population has the same formal status as any other group. Chicanos constitute an internal colony because they are legal citizens occupying a status of formal equality although informally their status is one of inequality.

Richard Burkey (1978) maintains that a system of dominance evolves over time. Chicano historian Alberto Camarillo (1979) agrees, and has documented the creation of a California barrio as a historical process of deterioration, economic control, and racial discrimination. My own barrio study, *Bessemer* (1988), was somewhat unlike Camarillo's in that the nature and character of it were strongly defined by Colorado Fuel and Iron's Sociological Department. Nevertheless, it also is characterized by a historical process of deterioration, economic control, and racial discrimination. Like other U.S. barrios, from its conception Bessemer has been, and continues to be, a community distinct from the larger community. It is what Erving Goffman (1961) would call a total institution. From the beginning most barrios have been self-contained. The steel mill is no longer a controlling factor and the work force has been drastically reduced, but the barrio is still a psychological and social concept. In the minds of Bessemer barrio residents, it is a definite area with certain kinds of people having definite characteristics: It is a low-income, deteriorating area inhabited primarily by Chicanos. Its counterpart is the black ghetto.

There are interrelated factors that keep people from leaving barrios, but they do not work in isolation. There is interaction between outside forces and the desire not to venture outside the barrio because of harsh treatment. Residential arrangements are not haphazard and formless. W. Lloyd Warner and Leo Srole (1945) noted that they have a clear-cut, pervasive order and pattern, and are significantly similar in more general characteristics that serve to attract individuals similar in status to those already living in the area. These features have maintained barrios and ghettos separate from one another and from the dominant Anglo population.

A point of disagreement is with Barrera's contention that Anglo-Chicano relations began with the Mexican-American War of 1846. Southwestern Anglo-Hispanic relations began earlier. In Colorado they began as early as 1806, when Zebulon Pike was captured by the Spanish while he trespassed on Spanish territory. Long before this, Mexicans and Anglos traded in Santa Fe and Taos, New Mexico. Other examples of early Mexican and American relations exist in California, Arizona, and Texas. What is significant about the Mexican-American War is that its end made the Mexicans a conquered population. Sociologist Richard Burkey (1978) maintains that relationships characterized by conquest always set in motion dominant-subordinate relationships. Although Burkey also maintains that such beginnings can be identified with relative precision, it is not easy to establish when Anglo-Chicano relations began and when they became antagonistic. Most early documentation available in America was written by white Americans, and Anglo writers did not always accurately record information, in many instances twisting the truth.

After the war the conflicts continued. The *Rocky Mountain News* (1979) reported that from 1870 to 1874, Colorado territorial legislator Felipe Baca (Baca was former Colorado senator Polly Baca's great-great uncle) actively opposed Colorado statehood because it would allow the northern territory, with a well-financed Anglo population, to dominate the southern territory, where Hispanics had controlled the land for generations but had little capital. Such Anglo-Chicano conflict exists today but at another level, as evidenced by the language used by each group to describe the other. Anglos refer to Chicanos as "greasers," "spicks," "beaners," and "taco benders." Chicanos refer to Anglos as "gringos," "rednecks," "peckers," and "honkies."

The internal colonial model contends that the dominant group carries out deliberate policies to constrain, transfer, or destroy the native population's values, orientations, and ways of life. Negative stereotypes are advanced in an attempt to discredit the population and make them feel ashamed of their ways, manners, traditions, values, and language. Chicanos have reported that "no speaking Spanish" rules in schools and businesses were officially encountered as late as 1968. At an official level many of those rules continue today. Converting non-English-speaking people into English-speakers was one of the primary objectives of U.S. schools.

Barrera (1979) proposes that a systesm of structural discrimination exists initially in the economic sector of a society and then spreads to other areas. In the Gunnar Myrdal (1944) tradition this creates a vicious cycle of poverty in which the minority is trapped in a powerless position. A missing factor is social-psychological oppression. Together this limits competition for employment, education, political power, and health. It allows privileges and status to those not discriminated against and builds racism into the ongoing process. Discrimination, via racism and sexism, begins at the cognitive level with misconceived perceptions by the two groups about each other. In the tradition of Frantz Fanon (1963) and Albert Memmi (1965), the dominant group sets itself up as the most worthy group because it shows physical/material evidence of its worthiness and possesses enough social control to tell the subordinate group about the dominant group's worthiness. The powerless minority may adopt or internalize this ideology. Perceptions shape a predisposition to act in a discriminatory manner.

Barrera (1979) extends Robert Blauner's (1969, 1972) casual mention that racial prejudice is largely a product of racial ideologies that were developed to justify structural discrimination. He incorporates historical works that demonstrate job competition, by Anglos and racial minorities, as increasing racial tension and prejudice. According to Barrera, antagonisms arose because institutionalized hiring practices attempted to undercut Anglo wages by creating a cheap Mexican labor pool. Anglo workers were angered because they saw Chicano workers as unfair competition, but rather than express hostility toward the controlling employer, they expressed hostility toward the more vulnerable and visible Chicano. Both populations' economic and social hostilities were transferred to the general community and a cycle of displaced discriminatory, hostile transference was set in motion.

Barrera (1979) and Muñoz (1972) do not agree on the sector of the society where discrimination begins. Muñoz contends it begins at the social-political level with conquest and negative stereotypes about the conquered. I tend to agree with Muñoz's somewhat ambivalent social-political origin. Conquest of the Mexicans was simultaneously political, social, and economic over a period of time, but it was also cultural and linguistic. My position is consistent with Hubert Blalock's (1967) contention that there is an interrelationship among variables that produce discrimination in a society.

Most of the scholarly consideration of discrimination and the Mexican American has been structural in nature. It has focused upon how social institutions discriminate against the Chicano. Negative stereotypes and prejudiced thoughts evolved into discriminatory behavior transferred to social institutions, making it most visible, but its most important toll was upon the economic sector. Conquest and discrimination are multidimensional phenomena at both the structural and the personal, psychological level.

DECOLONIZATION AS A MODEL FOR SOCIAL CHANGE

Barrio studies reveal that some Chicanos work within the system to modify it. Some criticize and attack the system from the outside. Others defend the system and are called "Coconut" or "Tio Taco." Most Chicanos do not passively accept injustices. They continue to create ways of dealing with the Anglo. The Chicano has developed the ability to respond to a concrete predicament. Rolando Juaquez (1976) defines this as interpreting and situating an individual within a conceptual scheme: People have to do what they must to survive. They very cautiously select moments and issues on which they must take a stand. This caution, I believe, fashions the Chicano way of life. Chicanos know from experience that relationships with Anglos can be painful and disadvantageous. This self-imposed behavior limits economic competition. It also limits other opportunities and confines the Chicano to the barrio. This action, coupled with institutional discrimination, fixates the Chicano in the barrio. When viewed from an outside perspective, the Chicano may appear self-defeating, to suffer from loss of self-concept and self-esteem, but when viewed from the inside, the Chicano is highly motivated toward self-protection. This involves high self-esteem and a concept of self that connotes high self-worth.

Racism creates antagonisms and ambivalence. The Chicano feels an ambivalence and antagonism toward life outside the barrio. An- tagonisms are often felt toward Anglos simply because they are An- glo. There is also a basic antagonism to anything that is considered middle class. Anglo middle-class homes are felt to be uncomfortable. Sometimes these antagonisms are toward Chicanos who have adopted life-styles that are middle class or *agringado*. Middle-income Chicanos have had to face this contradiction.

Most Chicanos live in barrios, where they tolerate crowded con- ditions and what some Anglos would call deviant behavior. The local winos and junkies are examples of deviants living in, and being accepted by, the Chicano community. Although they are not courted, they are not treated badly or totally neglected. There seems to be a sense of understanding that they are not responsible for their condition. Many Chicanos would prefer to live in a part of town with better housing, but they also want to live with other Chicanos. Many choose to live in barrios even though they can afford to live elsewhere. This is not to minimize the fact that there is outside social pressure to keep the Chicano in the barrio; it is to point out that some Chicanos lives there out of choice. There are also Chicanos who are functioning very well outside the barrio but are still linked to it by working with its population. These people have combined higher education and knowledge of local history and contemporary conditions in an effort to assist others in bettering their life chances and to promote social change. They are at the forefront of changing the barrio and are engaged in a form of passive resistance.

The internal colonial model extends decolonization as a process by which to bring about resistance and social change. Chris Garcia and Rodolfo de la Garza (1977) interpret decolonization as a group- oriented drive to control their own lives through employing tactics that will change their situation by changing the system entirely. Some have interpreted this statement as a call for violent overthrow, but many Chicanos recognize limitations and potentials, and have chosen to work within the system. As Barrera (1979) points out, there are Chicanos in various income classes, but all Chicanos have a common denominator in their cultural heritage and the socially oppressed conditions from which they originate. This commonality allows Chi- canos from various backgrounds frequent contact and a sense of unity. This is an important factor because it allows community cohe- sion and a sense of intimacy, and attributes some resources to the barrio.

Children are highly valued, and the Chicano community does much to present positive messages to them. Community leaders encourage children to strive for a better life, to stay in school, and to enjoy safe recreation.

Barrera and Muñoz contend that Chicano liberation involves developing group consciousness and rejecting established conditions. Most Chicanos have not rejected the established social structure as a whole. Most exist in terms of an American capitalist perspective. Those with resources have very cautiously selected elements of capitalism they deem positive and have incorporated them into new lifestyles. Good mental and physical health, although formally linked to the "gringo" world, are seen as valuable for the Chicano, but the Chicano needs a balance of factors from his own world. Chicano professionals are attempting to develop policies and programs in the interest of Chicanos and are teaching other Chicanos to do the same. They have encountered extreme resistance. A few, more radical, Chicanos view the professionals as "sellouts," but more and more individuals are recognizing the forces at work and are quick to note who and what works on their behalf and who and what does not.

Muñoz points out that occasionally Chicanos are allowed to administer Chicanos, but such administrators are usually kept in subordinate positions and are persons accepted as nonthreatening to the Anglo elite. For some Chicanos this is an ongoing contradiction, one that each person resolves individually.

There is a new psychology, a new ideology, forming and advancing from the barrio. It is consistent with decolonization as proposed by Chicano scholars. It is a way of thinking about the Chicano condition through new ways of addressing the issues. The internal colonial model does not serve well to explain or change the psychology of the Chicano: what is thought, how it is thought, and what influence these factors have upon daily life. Internal colonialism assumes that changes at the institutional level will affect individuals at the personal level. No doubt they will, to an extent, but this takes away from Chicanos the ability to think and act on their own behalf, in their own interest, not only at the institutional level but also at a very personal level. Chicanos reveal this ability. The forces at work against them are still great, but the ideology previously outlined in this chapter is now the ruling individual ideology.

Barrera and Muñoz's internal colonial model does not allow for prediction past decolonization. Barrera casually mentions that class differences will become pronounced. The study of a working-class barrio can give us some answers to the question of the future of Chicanos. It is the future of these people that concerns some of the professional class.

The barrio can be a nice place, but it can also be a depressing place. It is limited in what it can offer individuals, and people know there is another society that has benefits to offer. The fact that the Anglo has control over these resources does not mean they are bad. Chicano youths are very much aware of the other society; they see it in movies, on television, in newspapers and magazines. They fear that this society is off limits. Many of them kill or control the desire for new cars, better homes, clothes, and vacations by rationalizing that these things are "gringo." Some work and save to afford the best brand name. Some exert extraordinary pressure on parents to provide these articles. Media advertising supports this. Sometimes youth create alternatives. They reject the style and dress as *cholos* and *cholas* in working-class attire. This clothing is not always cheaper, but it is of better quality and it makes a political statement: "I am Chicano and I have an ideology." To compensate for not owning new automobiles, they customize late model, mid-priced automobiles. This symbol of status is mobile. "Lowriding" compensates for low-quality housing, crowded conditions, and lack of economic and political opportunity.

The future of the Chicano is difficult to predict because the population is so diverse. The future is also difficult to predict in isolation from the rest of America. What happens in the United States will surely affect the lives of Chicanos. A more rational approach would be an attempt to predict the future of a class of people in relationship to people of the dominant culture in the same class. If current efforts are maintained, and greater numbers of the Chicano population achieve the status of the current professional class, I believe the Chicanos will adhere to Chicano cultural ways while taking advantage of those resources they now lack. This means Chicanos will be bicultural and will have a better living standard. Chicanos are returning to the use of their Spanish language and are attempting to reinstate family ties and cultural ways. They do this at the same time they visit the dentist, have yearly health examinations, attend the universities, and campaign for political office.

Although the internal colonial model has limitations, it also has some advantages. It is of broad scope, allowing for the analysis of Anglo and Chicano race relations. It is historical, and it is contemporary. Criticism has been advanced by Fred Cervantes (1973) in regard to the failure of the model to account for some institutions responding to Chicano issues. Cervantes assumes institutions initiated the positive response. They did not. Chicanos fought to participate in them, and they continue to fight to remain active in them. Cervantes states that internal colonialism does not give sufficient direction to promote social change; I contend that it does. Social change has taken place over a short period of time and continues to take place. Since the 1960s social change has occurred for some Chicanos at an extremely rapid pace. In the 1960s a Chicano middle class was impossible to talk about. It is only in retrospect that significant change can be measured. Thus, the social-historical approach is appropriate in the long run. It is not difficult to assess whether the forces of Chicano social action are the negation of internal colonialism. Social action taken since the 1960s has been toward this end. It is a continual process with no distinct bench mark to announce its end.

Cervantes also questions whether racism is a function of colonialism or an operational part of it. Racism is the means of social, cultural, economic, and political control. It serves to keep populations from gaining access to resources and privileges by placing physical, structural, and individual constraints upon them. It defines a definite physical, social, and psychological space for people. It is an operational part of colonialism. Cervantes and many others have a problem with the term "colonialism." I do not. Cleaning up the language to placate some would gloss over discrimination and its historical and contemporary context. However, a discussion on sexism is warranted. Racism and sexism are types of discrimination. The internal colonial model does not discuss sexism. Both minority males and females experience both racism and sexism. To envelop these phenomena I suggest the term "multidimensional or multifaceted discrimination": discrimination that takes place in education, economics, politics, and health care, and that is directed at both males and females. It must be understood that the internal colonial model is but a step in creating a more appropriate theory by which to understand the Chicano community experience.

THE LANGUAGE OF SOCIAL CHANGE

Alongside theories explaining social deviance are theories explaining social change. The modernist perspective is concerned with labeling. Labeling theory alerts us to how some groups are given the label "deviant" for advocating social change. Some aspects of this theory have already been discussed in my focus on the definers and the defined, but labeling theory concerns itself with how the label or labels become shared by the deviants (the defined) and the conformists (the definers). This study also concerns itself with the outcome of the above relationship. Like other sociological theories, it assumes that deviance is culturally relative, and that what is important is the interpretation given to the label (Becker 1963). This can be extended to mean that the label carries worth. If one is labeled negatively in the hierarchically structured English language, one carries negative worth. More frequently than not, labels are agents of direct social control. Researchers, the media, the police, probation and parole officers, teachers, scientists, doctors, and social workers use labels to categorize and inadvertently stigmatize the labeled.

Chicanos have also been labeled negatively because they are descendants of the people who lost the racist Mexican-American War;

they have been labeled "losers." Everything that is Mexican has been devalued in America. When white Americans tell the story of the Mexican-American War, it is told so that Americans look glorious. They make heroes of Davey Crockett and Jim Bowie, vicious, unethical racists who killed for money. The Anglo legend of the Alamo is deceiving. It leads one to believe the Alamo was a large, very important Mexican mission. It is not very large, and it was only one of several missions. One is disappointed upon visiting the Alamo in San Antonio. Controlling forces have proceeded with little attention to the fact that for Mexican Americans a Catholic mission is a sacred place even if it has been desanctified. A visit to the Alamo never reveals that Davey Crockett did not emerge from the Alamo victorious. One is left with the image that he single-handedly won the war by knocking Mexicans off the mission wall with the butt of his rifle after he ran out of ammunition. In fact, Crockett was taken prisoner and later executed by the Mexicans.

Chicano and black studies have contributed much to the clarification of American reality, but they have been suppressed academic endeavors. They, like women's studies, had to force their knowledge onto university and college campuses, and they have not been granted full academic legitimization out of fear that their perspective will embarrass the legitimate disciplines. These studies have been labeled "radical," "critical," and "unscientifically grounded" without acknowledging that they are the newest American addition to a broad body of knowledge. Chicano studies is at the forefront of American scholarship and is being recognized in Central and Latin America, and in Europe. Yet it is suppressed in order to maintain the status quo and to control both the minority and the majority populations. Those in control do not want the truth to be known. It threatens white privilege.

The system of institutionalized discrimination feeds itself. Because it is supported in the social institutions, it gives itself life. This model expands on Myrdal's (1944) cycle of poverty and asserts that racism penetrates not only social institutions but also the thoughts of individuals who compose the society. The invisible control of thoughts takes place at the ideological level. If white Americans accept a contention that white is superior, and everything around them sustains this, they will believe they are superior and act accordingly. If Chicanos are given messages that they are inferior, they may internalize that they are inferior and act accordingly. But social scientists have informed us that the faction being attributed negative value does not always believe the attributor. The Chicano-Anglo experience shows this to be true. Chicanos have not totally accepted negative messages about themselves. This is why they continue to struggle to maintain their identity.

There are other elements of social control in the barrio. Easily recognized is the number of police officers in the area. Chicanos generally have negative relationships with police officers. Anglo authority and its representatives have been looked upon with disgust since the early days of the Texas Rangers. Police presence in the barrios threatens Chicanos and keeps them conscious that they are being watched, that their civil liberties are not always protected, and that they may be victimized. Chicanos have had a violent historical relationship with representatives of white authority. The *Corrido de Gregorio Cortez* (Paredes 1958) is a wonderful insight into Chicano-police relations and how the community has documented atrocities and injustices. Other early victims of Anglo policing were Joaquín Murieta, Juan "Cheno" Cortinas, the Espinoza brothers of southern Colorado, and the Gorras Blancas and Hermanos Penitentes of New Mexico.

Chicanos have traditionally resisted Anglo oppression. In response, Anglo-controlled media have made them appear as social bandits. Social bandits are heroes to Chicanos and bandits to Anglos. Public sentiment, both Anglo and Chicano, has been manipulated against Chicanos who resist. Textbooks, TV, and newspapers tend to present only the Anglo perspective or totally exclude the truth from both Anglos and Chicanos. This has an impact on socialization that takes places at various levels: via education and the media, through policing and laws, even through religion, the family, and, especially, ideology and language.

Language can also be used as a form of social control. Spanish-speaking individuals incur severe negative social consequences for speaking Spanish. In school some are told to speak English; at home, parents want children to speak English so they can succeed in school, in employment, in society. Chicanos love their children and do not want them subjected to the negative consequences they endured for speaking what is not, but is called, a "foreign" language.

In the past some parents did not speak Spanish to their children. They kept the language from them. When they did use the language, they used it as a secret code. When this is done, children become threatened by their own language. They grow to dislike it and even block it out. When they are older, they may desire to learn Spanish but cannot. Some know they know how to speak Spanish, but their mouths will not do what they know in their mind they can do. These passive bilingual (monolingual, English-speaking) Chicanos only need social permission to speak Spanish. With social permission they quickly regain their language. What has happened is that youth and Chicanos of other ages have been subjected to such social control, such psychological violence, that they have developed psychological blocks as protective mechanisms.

The reacquisition of language is essential for the restoration of both power and culture. With linguistic power one retains culture because culture is structured as language is structured. If English, a tremendously value-laden, hierarchically structured language, is used, there will result a similarly structured culture. If a more laterally structured language is used, there will result a more laterally structured and egalitarian culture. One can immediately recognize the tendencies for cultural conflict. Spanish- and English-speaking cultures frequently think and act in opposite manners.

SUMMARY

Resistance to Anglo social control is included in Chicano ideology. The study of contemporary Chicano cultural productions, such as art and music, reveals aspects of this ideology. Long-standing traditions include music and mural art. Mural art was used by Diego Rivera, José Orozco, David Siqueiros, and others during the Mexican Revolution to educate masses of illiterate people. During the Chicano civil rights movement of the 1960s, mural art experienced a rebirth in the United States. Chicanos drew upon the Mexican tradition to educate barrio people politically. Although American barrio people were slightly more literate than their Mexican ancestors, they were rather unsophisticated about the nature of oppression. The arts— music, murals, literature, theater, and poetry—educated them about their history in the United States. Chicanos continue to nurture themselves and to rely on their culture to provide positive self-images. However, without planned urbanization, the dominant cultural values are incorporated into Chicanos' culture and into their psyches. Chicanos have been encouraged to investigate and articulate their ideology, the psychology and the philosophy of racism. They need to understand the racist mind. They need to understand the sexist mind. The difference between the two is the victim. Racism and sexism are the same thing: discrimination.

The understanding of an ideology that discriminates against people of color is extended as one based on inappropriate feelings of superiority. A focus on the work of George Herbert Mead (1934), who emphasized the significance of getting "under the skin" of others by taking their roles, enables one to better understand the impact of social control on the Chicano.

Children, for example, internalize the roles of their parents and significant others. They model their behavior after them and incorporate parental values, attitudes, and norms into their personality. As they grow older, they come into contact with others who have had similar or different socialization. These people represent the society as a whole, "generalized others." In interacting with the attitudes of generalized others, the child internalizes the values of the society.

Children learn that life has rules when they play games with rules. For Mead, internalized values are only one part of the personality. Another part consists of spontaneous, creative, or impulsive behavior. This part is more individualized. It suffices to say that parents are important people in the lives of white American children as well as of Chicano children. We conclude that Chicano and white children have different experiences because they are born to parents who are culturally different. Mead's contention that children learn the rules of society when they play games with rules shows that most games reflect the culture of their production.

In tracing Chicano children's development, I have focused on the kind of play in which they engage. At this time my attention is on the fact that Chicanos learn Chicano cultural rules first, between the ages of birth and 5; and when they go to school, from ages 5 to 18, they learn Anglo rules. These rules frustrate, punish, and attempt to give the child a negative image of his cultural self, his culture, and his people. After the age of 18, the Chicano is left to fend for himself/herself, mostly unaware of the nature of America's unwritten, unstated rules.

REFERENCES

Acuna, Rodolfo. 1972. *Occupied America: The Struggle Toward Chicano Liberation*. San Francisco: Canfield.

————. 1981. *Occupied America: A History of Chicanos.* New York: Harper and Row. 2d ed. of *Occupied America* (1972).

Barrera, Mario. 1979. *Race and Class in the Southwest.* South Bend, IN: University of Notre Dame Press.

Becker, Howard S. 1963. *Outsiders: Studies in the Sociology of Deviance.* New York: Free Press.

Blalock, Hubert M., Jr. 1967. *Toward a Theory of Minority Group Relations.* New York: Capricorn Books.

Blauner, Robert. 1969. "Internal Colonialism and Ghetto Revolt." *Social Problems* 16 (Spring): 393–408.

————. 1972. *Racial Oppression in America.* New York: Harper and Row.

Blea, Irene I. 1988. *Bessemer: A Sociological Perspective of a Chicano Barrio.* New York: AMS Press.

Burkey, Richard. 1978. *Ethnic and Racial Groups: The Dynamics of Dominance.* Menlo Park, CA: Benjamin/Cummings.

Camarillo, Alberto. 1979. *Chicanos in a Changing Society.* Cambridge, MA: Harvard University Press.

Cervantes, Fred A. 1973. "Chicanos as a Post-Colonial Minority: Some Questions Concerning the Adequacy of the Paradigm of Internal Colonialism." In *Perspectives in Chicano Studies.* Los Angeles: Chicano Studies Publications.

Durkheim, Emile. 1966. *Suicide,* J. Spaulding and George Simpson, trans. New York: Free Press. Original work published 1897.

Fanon, Frantz. 1963. *The Wretched of the Earth.* New York: Grove Press.

García, F. Chris, and Rodolfo de la Garza. 1977. *The Chicano Political Experience: Three Perspectives.* North Scituate, MA: Duxberry Press.

Goffman, Erving. 1961. *Asylum.* Chicago: Aldine.

Hirschi, Travis. 1969. *Causes of Delinquency.* Berkeley: University of California Press.

Juaquez, Rolando A. 1976. "What the Tape Recorder Has Created: A Broadly Based Exploration into Contemporary Oral History Practice." *Aztlan: International Journal of Chicano Studies* 2 (Spring): 12–16.

Krohn, Marvin D., and James L. Massey. 1980. "Social Control and Delinquent Behavior: An Examination of the Social Bond." *Sociological Quarterly* 21 (Autumn): 529–43.

————. 1980. "Social Status and Deviance." *Criminology* 18: 303–18.

Mead, George Herbert. 1934. *Mind, Self and Society: The Standpoint of a Behaviorist,* Charles W. Morris, ed. Chicago: University of Chicago Press.

Memmi, Albert. 1965. *The Colonizer and the Colonized.* Boston: Beacon Press.

Merton, Robert K. 1957. *Social Theory and Social Structure,* pp. 185–248. New York: Free Press.

Mirande, Alfredo. 1985. *The Chicano Experience.* South Bend, IN: University of Notre Dame Press.

Muñoz, Carlos, Jr. 1972. *The Politics of Urban Protest: A Model of Political Analysis.* Claremont, CA: Graduate School of Government.

Myrdal, Gunnar. 1944. *American Dilemma.* New York: Harper.

Nye, F. Ivan. 1958. *Family Relationships and Delinquent Behavior.* New York: Wiley.

Paredes, Américo. 1958. *With a Pistol in His Hand: A Border Ballad and Its Hero.* Austin: University of Texas Press.

Reckless, Walter C. 1973. *The Crime Problem.* 5th ed. New York: Appleton-Century-Crofts.

Rocky Mountain News. 1979. Denver, May 6.

Scamehorn, H. Lee. 1966. *Pioneer of the West.* Boulder, CO: Pruett.

Sutherland, Edwin H. 1961. *White Collar Crime.* New York: Holt, Rinehart and Winston.

Warner, W. Lloyd, and Leo Srole. 1945. *The Social Systems of American Ethnic Groups.* New Haven: Yale University Press.

Wiatrowski, Michael D., David B. Griswold, and Mary K. Roberts. 1981. "Social Control Theory and Delinquency." *American Sociological Review* 46 (October): 525–41.

6
Electoral and Nonelectoral Politics

INTRODUCTION

Although civil rights for Chicanos have advanced, the basic power structure in the country has not changed. People who have money and political power control society. For this reason, one of the most important contemporary Chicano issues is political participation. Other issues are economic development, education, the promotion of Chicano artistic productions, and better health, housing, and protection under the law. However, Chicanos do not see these issues as separate from political power.

Historically, power holders have maintained their control by keeping Chicanos, women, and other minorities disinfranchised from the political process. Earlier in history Chicanos were either intentionally excluded from political participation or inadvertently neglected. Today some of this practice of exclusion and neglect is more subtle, but it continues. Therefore, Chicanos openly assert their right to participate.

In spite of the media attention given to the Hispanic vote, some Chicanos do not know how to access political participation. Thus, much effort has been put into ensuring not only access but also viable participation at the decision-making level of the two major parties, in the caucuses, and in the infrastructure of the parties.

TWO KINDS OF POLITICS

Chicano attention to politics has been divided into two efforts: nonelectoral and electoral politics. Before the Great Depression, organizations such as the Hermanos Penitentes, the Orden de Hijos de América (Order of Sons of America, 1921–1929), and the League of United Latin American Citizens (1929) were already founded. Many efforts to empower the Chicano community had taken place in union organization, and many community organizations, such as La Zaragoza in Pueblo, Colorado (1919), already existed. The Hermanos Penitentes, of New Mexico, were probably among the first to organize for political purposes. However, that brotherhood does not appear to have entered into political causes and other nonreligious issues after its initial involvement.

Members of early organizations were exclusively Chicanos with minimal economic stability. Their intentions were to address Chicano issues of education, political participation, and upward mobility. Most of their early efforts were in the area of nonelectoral politics. Access and retention of education tended to be a primary focus. Their early impact was not immediately felt throughout the Southwest. Their concerns were originally local concerns.

The League of United Latin American Citizens (LULAC) began as an apolitical organization, but today it is one of the most powerful organizations in the nation. LULAC was originally mainstream in orientation. It sought to promote the advancement of Chicanos in traditional Anglo society. It was apprehensive of negative responses by Anglos. Because of this apprehension, it refused to organize a drive for poll tax payment and voter registration (Garcia and De la Garza 1977). Today it is at the forefront in addressing Chicano issues. LULAC was and is a reformist organization. World War II was a great blow to the reform movement because many of its leaders were male, were on active duty in the U.S. Army, and were killed.

The war, however, allowed Chicano men to be exposed to new opportunities. These opportunities were manifested in some entry into jobs and institutions that had been virtually closed to them prior to the war. The war also brought limited opportunity for some women to enter the labor market. The new opportunities were brought about by the American male labor shortage, and quickly closed when males returned from the war. The worker shortage was one of the main reasons for initiation of the 1942 version of the bracero program, which legally brought guest workers from Mexico into the United States.

Chicanos were one of the most decorated ethnic groups in World War II. Some 350,000 Chicanos served in the armed forces. Seventeen of them were awarded the Medal of Honor (Thernstrom 1980). Yet during the war there were race riots in the streets of Los Angeles. American military men harassed and beat Chicano "zoot suit" youth. This was the era of the *pachuco* and *pachuca*. At the end of the war, Chicanos were faced with de facto exclusion from public facilities, education, jury duty, and political participation. World War II veterans were not allowed to join Veterans of Foreign Wars posts. The dead were not allowed burial in Arlington National Cemetery. Some Chicanos had to file lawsuits to gain their military benefits. They demanded fair treatment based upon their military participation.

This post-World War II experience changed the Chicano condition in a way that had never been felt before. Some Chicano organizations were founded in this new era. Chicano veterans formed the G.I. Forum in Texas. Unlike LULAC, the G.I. Forum began to openly challenge discrimination against Chicanos by the Veterans Administration. Later it expanded its involvements. Dr. Hector García led the organization. He dedicated his efforts to increasing Chicano voter registration and participation. The organization came to have branches in 23 states and more than 20,000 members. In California, a related event took place. Saul Alinsky established the Community Service Organization (CSO) in 1947. The CSO was to put pressure on local officials to improve housing, health services, and police activities. It was relatively successful, particularly in the Los Angeles area. The organization raised issues of interest to Chicanos for the next 30 years.

In 1958, the Mexican American Political Association (MAPA) was founded in California. Although MAPA was designed as an independent political organization, it supported the Democratic party until 1970. In Texas, the Political Association of Spanish Speaking Organizations (PASSO) included a larger base with non-Chicano membership. PASSO was extremely successful in electing local Chicano officials, especially in Crystal City in 1963.

Political organization included efforts to empower citizens beyond the voting booth. During the early 1960s Alinsky's efforts were badly needed and were supported by Chicano activists. These efforts further combined political participation and nonelectoral politics. They were also consistent with the civil rights movement and the involvement of poor people in addressing issues of poverty in America.

THE CHICANO MOVEMENT

The Chicano movement in the 1960s was a landmark Chicano experience. It became a dynamic force for social change. By the middle 1960s a conventional approach to social and political change had produced little benefit to Chicanos. Their average economic and educational levels were much lower than those of the Anglos. Chicanos knew they were suffering from discrimination and proceeded to take a more confrontational approach to their involvement. This approach included open criticism, protest marches, boycotts, sit-ins, and the use of the media.

During the 1960s many social movements were taking place. Black militants and Martin Luther King, Jr., and his nonviolent approaches were active. The women's movement was busy again. The predominantly white hippie movement criticized the American norm and the anti-Vietnam War protests were heated. Indeed, it was a heated time in America, and Chicanos and Chicanas were involved, to some degree, in all of these movements; but most of their energy was devoted to their own issues.

The movement was not monolithic but an amalgam of many incidents, individuals, and organizations coming together to improve the Chicano condition. The movement had a great impact on the development of Chicanismo, the articulated ideological feeling and political understanding of being Mexican American. This included political activism and cultural and ethnic pride (García and De la Garza 1977). The strategy employed in the development of this Chicano ideology was incorporated into murals, music, theater, and poetry.

During the Chicano movement, some leaders emphasized the appeals of Chicanismo. Physical expressions such as thrusting a fist and fully extended arm into the air and yelling "Chicano Power!" were seen and heard around the nation. This and other expressions symbolized Chicano pride and resistance to Anglo domination. These expressions sought equality, justice, and freedom as they are promised in America.

One leader who came to national attention was Rodolfo "Corky"

Gonzales. Gonzales had much influence among urban Chicanos, especially the youth, in Colorado and throughout the country. His epic poem "Yo Soy Joaquín" is monumental. Gonzales organized Los Voluntarios in Denver to demonstrate against police brutality in 1963. Although he became a director of one of the War on Poverty's youth programs, poverty officials thought that "Corky," as he came to be known, was too zealous in his defense of the Chicano community and fired him. In 1966 he established the Crusade for Justice, which has provided legal, medical, educational, civil rights, and financial services to Chicanos. He marched, supported student walkouts, and developed an alternative school, Escuela Tlatelolco, in the heart of Denver. Gonzales and his members of the Crusade for Justice knew Chicanos and Chicano culture. Their approach was multifaceted. They included the Catholic Church in their strategy. Members of the Crusade for Justice were instrumental in getting Spanish incorporated into the mass. In Colorado it was the Crusade for Justice that first openly advocated involvement in electoral politics via the La Raza Unida party.

Another leader of the time was José Angel Gutiérrez. He and his students formed the Mexican-American Youth Organization (MAYO) at St. Mary's College in San Antonio, Texas, in 1967. His approach was to confront the Anglo establishment and force it to include Chicanos. Under the Freedom of Information Act, he obtained documentation proving that the FBI had spied on organizations such as LULAC and the G.I. Forum. He and several other leaders spoke at rallies and conferences, and used the media. He spoke agaist police brutality and advocated political organization, warning: "We are fed up. We are going to move to do away with the injustices to the Chicano and if the 'gringo' doesn't get out of our way, we stampede over him" (Acuna 1981, p. 361). The Anglo establishment became hostile, especially when Gutiérrez and his supporters emerged with La Raza Unida as an alternative political party.

Reis Lopes Tijerina was one of the charismatic leaders of the Chicano movement. When he studied Bill Mundy, a rich agriculturalist in New Mexico, and other Anglos who had robbed the Mexicans of their land, he became interested in the land-grant issue. He was convinced that, according to the Treaty of Guadalupe Hidalgo, the national forest in Tierra Amarilla County belonged to Chicanos. This land was appropriated by the U.S. government. Originally it was communal land granted to the people of the area under Spanish and Mexican land-grant policy. It was not to be bought or sold as private property.

Tijerina established La Alianza in order to guarantee honoring of the Treaty of Guadalupe Hidalgo and called for the return of the land. In 1966, he and 350 supporters of La Alianza occupied national forest campgrounds to assert their right to the land. After a few days of occupation, state police, sheriff's deputies, and Texas Rangers attempted to displace them. La Alianza members placed two Rangers in confinement and brought them to trial for trespassing and being a public nuisance. Tijerina was arrested and sent to trial. He was sentenced to two years in prison with five years' probation. After he had stood trial several times, he tried to occupy another campground in the national forest. He was later charged with "aiding and abetting the destruction of U.S. Forest Service signs and assaulting and threatening a federal agent." The sentence was three years' confinement in the federal penitentiary. Tijerina's family and friends were always at his side. The unresolved issues still fester.

Another Chicano movement leader is César Chávez, who moved from San José to Delano, California, and began to organize farm laborers in 1962. By 1965 he had mobilized the United Farm Workers (UFW). By 1972 there were over 30,000 members and Chávez was affiliated with the AFL-CIO. The UFW succeeded in making strict agreements regarding growers' use of dangerous pesticides and collective-bargaining legislation. Chávez and his workers implemented strikes, boycotts, and marches, and took a nonviolent strategy as devout Roman Catholics.

Chávez's strategies were rooted in the tactics of Saul Alinsky, who gained a reputation for mobilizing and politicizing previously disenfranchised groups. Using Alinsky's tactics, Chávez assisted farm workers prosecuted for trying to obtain just treatment from the establishment. He developed strategies for getting people out of jail, settling immigration problems, and getting driver's licenses. Organizer Dolores Huerta, who was born in Ratón, New Mexico, was, and continues to be, a viable part of the UFW efforts. Like Chávez, she uses the existing laws and the perspective that groups can undermine the authority by pointing out that the authority does not obey its own laws, that it applies it laws selectively, and that people have power if they organize. The UFW drew the attention of the mass media by creating demonstrations such as the march to Sacramento of 1966. Although this tactic was both popular and effective in the 1960s and 1970s, in the 1980s it is less effective.

Today the active leaders and organizations that were seen in the 1960s and the early 1970s have faded away but have not disappeared. La Raza Unida's party ideology lives on. The party motivated and achieved effective control of local school boards and city governments in some rural and smaller urban areas. Its demands are still voiced, and similar activities continue in different forms. Many activists once in La Raza Unida are today's major participants in the Democratic and the Republican parties.

ELECTORAL POLITICS

Despite the projection that they will soon be the largest U.S. minority, Hispanics hold a relatively small proportion of decision-making power and are a small part of the total national electorate. Gathering statistics is difficult because of inconsistent data. According to the U.S. Census, Hispanic citizens of voting age compose only 4.2 percent of the total voting age citizens, whereas the Hispanic population is 6.4 percent of the total population. This population figure is misleading. There is a higher proportion of noncitizens and undocumented workers among Hispanics. Seventy percent of Hispanic adults were estimated to be citizens in 1980, compared with 97 percent of the total U.S. population (U.S. Bureau of the Census 1984). This makes estimating the true number of Hispanics in the United States difficult. In fact, estimates range from 12 million to 20 million in the U.S. population.

Hispanics tend to be younger than non-Hispanics. The median age for Hispanics was 22.1 years in 1980, while that of non-Hispanics was 31. The number of Hispanics of voting age becomes a crucial issue for those wanting to predict and address the concerns of Hispanics via political participation. As the Anglo population gets older and dies, the Chicano population also gets older, and can be in a position to have a more profound influence on the decisions that give direction to the United States. Some Anglos worry that Chicanos might not treat them very well.

Hispanics have the capability of strong voting power, especially since their population is concentrated in several states. Eighty-five percent of voting age Hispanics reside in the nine states of California, Texas, New York, Florida, Illinois, New Jersey, New Mexico, Arizona, and Colorado. Thus, political participation, next to education, becomes a priority. The 9 states have a total of 193 electoral votes, 71 percent of the 270 votes needed to elect a president of the United States.

Chicanos comprise approximately 60 percent of the U.S. Hispanic population and are especially concentrated in the five states of New Mexico, California, Texas, Arizona, and Colorado. This is the area lost to the United States by Mexico at the end of the Mexican-American war, and these are the states in which Chicano-Anglo relations are perhaps the most antagonistic.

RECENT ELECTORAL POLITICS

Until the late 1970s, Chicano voters had been ignored in national elections. The presidential election of 1960 was the only exception. During that election, the Democrats and John F. Kennedy courted the Chicano community. This happened primarily because Chicanos and the Chicano movement were receiving much media attention and raising the race relations consciousness of the nation. The Democratic effort to attract Chicanos was successful, and Kennedy received 85 percent of the Chicano vote.

In New Mexico and Texas, where Kennedy could not receive a majority of the Anglo vote, the Chicano vote became vital. The Chicano vote also gave Kennedy a majority in New Mexico, where he won by a 2000-vote margin. He carried Texas with 91 percent of the Chicano vote (Velásquez 1986).

The 1964 and 1968 elections, however, revealed a weakness in Chicano voting influence. This was due to low voter participation. During the presidential election of 1972, Chicanos and other politicians were aware of their fragmented and weakened condition but were not able to mobilize to make an impact. That year Chicanos were not eagerly courted by the Democratic party.

During the late 1970s and the 1980s, Chicanos made significant gains in politics. The gains were realized between 1978 and 1982. Leading the way were the Southwest and the Midwest Voter Registration Projects, which registered over a million Latino voters. The impact was felt in cities across the nation. In Chicago, Latino coalitions with blacks and progressive whites elected Harold Washington, a black man, mayor. Miami saw major changes in its political

Table 1
Hispanic Voting Age Population and Electoral Votes in a Nine-State Area

STATE	NUMBER	% OF TOTAL VOTING AGE POPULATION	NUMBER OF ELECTORAL VOTES
California	2,775,170	16.1	47
Texas	1,756,170	17.7	29
New York	1,061,852	8.3	36
Florida	629,292	8.5	21
Illinois	379,208	4.6	24
New Jersey	307,321	5.7	16
New Mexico	292,714	33.1	5
Arizona	256,688	13.3	7
Colorado	204,301	9.8	8
Subtotal	7,663,517	11.6	193
U.S. Total	8,980,717	5.5	539

Source: The Hispanic Electorates (San Antonio, TX: Southwest Voter Education Project, 1984).

structure, and Florida was the first state to face the "English as official language" issue.

In the Republican party, Chicanos had not been a major national influence, but they had been at the state and local level, especially in New Mexico. New Mexico has a unique Republican voting record. Much of this is rooted in early political organizing done by the Penitente brotherhood in order to promote Chicano political, cultural, and ethnic domination in the area.

In 1976, the Chicano vote gave Jimmy Carter significant margins in Texas and Ohio. Carter also won in Texas, where Chicanos gave him a margin of over 20,000 votes. He gathered 18,000 Hispanic, mainly Chicano and Puerto Rican, votes in Ohio and won by about 11,000 votes (Velásquez 1986).

The Chicano electorate attracts a great deal of attention in the national media, especially the print media (*Businessweek* 1983; *U.S. News & World Report* 1983; *New York Times* 1984; *Washington Post* 1986; *U.S.A. Today* 1985). In the 1980s, both the Democrats and the Republicans are making efforts to gain the Hispanic vote.

In response to Democrat success in obtaining Chicano support in 1976, Republicans created the Republican National Hispanic Assembly. In 1983, Republican President Ronald Reagan hosted a series of events to honor Hispanics at the White House. At this time he met with Hispanic educators, those in the armed forces, and GOP workers. He announced the appointment of Katharine Ortega as U.S. Secretary of the Treasury; three times in a single week, he spoke about his Hispanic efforts. He also announced economic assistance to the southern border states, which had been hit hard by the devaluation of the Mexican peso.

As a countermove, Democratic Senator Edward Kennedy of Massachusetts maintained that the Reagan administration was the most anti-Hispanic administration in history. Popular Chicano opinion is not generally favorable to the Republican party.

Nevertheless, Reagan received one-third of the Hispanic vote in 1984. The Republicans made the assumption that Hispanic support for President Reagan in 1984 gave them an opening. In April 1986, the Republicans tested print and radio advertisements in California, Texas, New Mexico, and Arizona prior to the Cinco de Mayo celebration. The May 5 celebration, Mexican Independence Day, is a very important political and cultural celebration for U.S. Chicanos. The Republicans realized that the Hispanic vote in those states could be crucial in the Senate and gubernatorial races in 1986, and by Election Day had allocated about $300,000 to their Hispanic project.

THE CURRENT STRATEGY

The obstacle to addressing Chicano issues through voting power is low participation. In 1982, for instance, only 52 percent of eligible Hispanic voters were registered, and only 37 percent of eligible Hispanics showed up at the polls (Brischetto and Velásquez 1983).

There are several reasons for the traditionally low participation of Chicanos. Historically, literacy tests and tests requiring voters to prove "good moral character" were used to keep minorities from voting. These tests were outlawed by the 1970 amendments to the Voting Rights Act. Residency laws have also worked hardships on Chicanos, especially migrant workers. Until recently, voter registration offices were open only on weekdays between 9 A.M. and 5 P.M. This made it difficult for working Chicanos, some of whom hold two jobs and who are more likely to vote, to register.

Another factor contributing to lack of Chicano participation is the felony laws. These laws, which take voting rights away from felons, negatively impact Chicanos, who are disproportionately represented in this category. Chris García and Rodolfo de la Garza maintain that "The fact that Chicanos are found in disproportionately high numbers among inmates of penitentiaries means that they are also disproportionately disenfranchised" (1977, p. 79). This disenfranchisement is multifaceted, and is exhibited as low health standards, low income, and low education at the same time it manifests itself in low political participation.

It should be noted that other socioeconomic factors coincide with higher or lower voting participation. Middle-aged people vote more often than the young or the very old. College graduates vote substantially more than people with high school or grade school education. People who have high incomes are more likely to vote than those who have low incomes. The socioeconomic characteristics of Chicanos, including their younger population, lower income, and less formal education, explain lower participation.

Another explanatory factor is that Chicanos do not trust the system to respond to their attempts at participation. Sociological predictions would assume that Chicanos will vote more often as their socioeconomic status increases. It is also possible that Chicanos will match non–Chicano participation levels because the total voting participation in the United States is substantially lower than in many other countries. In fact, only about 52 percent of eligible white voters went to the polls in the 1982 election.

The Chicano vote began to play a significant role in national elections of the 1980s, despite the low participation. This is largely due to the existence of a viable middle-income group and its links to working-class and lower-class Hispanics. This social-political link is highly crucial to Chicano political participation as a means of addressing Chicano concerns.

Nevertheless, the political situation for Chicanos is still far from equity. It is necessary to look into voter registration drives and the numbers of Chicano elected officials as two means by which to evaluate Chicano political power. In the 1980s several projects are in motion to increase the number of registered Hispanic voters and to continue to address Chicano issues.

The Southwest Voter Registration Education Project (SVREP) has labored to raise the level of Hispanic political participation throughout the Southwest since 1975. Between the 1976 and 1980 presidential elections, Mexican American registrations increased by 664,695 (Morgan 1983). Willie Velásquez, long time executive director of SVREP whose life ended due to cancer in 1988, reported that the project funded 24 registration campaigns in Texas, Arizona, New Mexico, California, and Colorado in 1983 and 1984. These campaigns added 443,689 Hispanic voters. SVREP's privately financed budget has grown from $67,000 in 1975 to nearly $1 million in 1985.

The votes of Hispanic women became important in the 1980s. During the 1970s the registration rate for Hispanic men remained about 5 percent higher than for Hispanic women, but by 1980 the rate for Hispanic women had caught up with that for Hispanic men. Members of the Mexican American Women's National Association participated in voter registration drives in Washington, D.C., Texas, Kansas, and New Mexico before the 1984 election. Other Hispanic organizations, such as the National Conference of Puerto Rican Women, the National Voter Participation Project, and the Women's Vote Project, contributed to increasing the Hispanic female voter registration (*Nuestro* 1984). All over the country women continue to address feminist as well as Chicano issues, and political participation is but one approach.

In the history of the United States, a female or a Chicano has not

Table 2
Hispanic Elected Officials by Party and State

NAME	*PARTY/STATE		DISTRICT
Henry B. Gonzales	D	– Texas	20
Solomon Ortiz	D	– Texas	27
Bill Richardson	D	– New Mexico	3
Matthew G. Martinez	D	– California	30
Esteban Torres	D	– California	34
Manuel Lujan	R	– New Mexico	1
Edward Roybal	D	– California	25
Eligio. "Kika" de la Garza	D	– Texas	15
Robert Garcia	D	– New York	18
Albert D. Bustamante	D	– Texas	23

*D = Democratic party.
R = Republican party.
Source: Martínez 1987.

been elected either president or vice-president of the country. There has been one Chicano U.S. senator since Joseph Montoya (D.-New Mexico) was defeated in 1976. The number of representatives, however, increased from four in 1977 to nine in 1983, and in the 1984 election, Albert Bustamente became the tenth Chicano congressman. As of 1985, Texas had four Chicano congressmen, California had three, New Mexico had two, and New York had one. Thus far, there have been no Chicana congresswomen. Although the number of Chicano congressmen has increased, Chicanos are still underrepresented.

According to Arthur Martínez (1979) there were 24 state senators in 1978, and 28 in 1986 (1987). The number of state representatives was 52 in 1978 and 59 in 1986. Outstanding increases are apparent in Arizona state senators (from 3 to 6), New Mexico state representatives (from 19 to 24), and Texas state representatives (from 15 to 21). There are two Chicanos—Raul Castro of Arizona and Jerry Apodaca of New Mexico—listed as state governors in 1979, but only one, Tony Anaya of New Mexico, in 1987.

The number of mayors in the five southwestern states increased during the period between 1977 and 1983. The number of mayors and vice-mayors in muncipalities with over 15,000 population in Arizona went from none to 2. In California, the number increased from 7 to 14 in municipalities with over 25,000 people; in Colorado, from 1 to 3 in municipalities with over 15,000; in Texas, from 3 to 5 in municipalities over 25,000.

Chicano mayors in two large cities are notable: Henry G. Cisneros was elected mayor of San Antonio in 1981, and Federico Peña of Denver was elected in 1983. Hispanic mayors have increased from 142 in 1985 to 183 in 1986 (*Hispanic Link* 1986a). Although the increases are encouraging Chicanos are still underrepresented.

Underrepresentation weakens the Chicano ability to address various issues. Major barriers also include gerrymandering and racial bias. Gerrymandering is the practice of dividing a geographical area into voting districts that give unfair advantage to one political party or group.

Gerrymandering has been the dominant barrier preventing Chicanos from winning elections in California. For example, as of 1970, the Chicano community in East Los Angeles, which had nearly a million Chicanos in population, was divided into nine state assembly districts and six U.S. congressional districts. The proportion of Chicanos in each district was kept below 40 percent, which meant the number of voters was insufficient to elect a Chicano representative.

At-large elections also work against Chicanos because they generally are concentrated in specific areas, barrios. In many cities they live in one area of town. At-large elections allow every eligible voter to vote, and Chicanos are generally outnumbered.

Racial bias has considerably affected the results of elections. Chicano candidates suffer bias, especially during runoffs. They are described in the press as representatives of a special interest group, while Anglo candidates are described as representatives of all the people. This bias causes Chicano candidates to lose non-Chicano votes.

A MULTIFACETED APPROACH TO ADDRESSING ISSUES

There appears to be little deviation from political participation as a vehicle by which to address Chicano issues. As the political situation changes, however, the strategy Chicanos take will also change. In the mid–1960s the political demands of Chicanos were radical. Since the late 1970s, however, nonelectoral politics are more moderate and institutionalized. There has been a move from a revolutionary to a reform model. The political field for Chicano activism has become local, state, and national elections. Before 1970 most Chicano efforts were at the local level. In the late 1980s Chicanos are uniting with other groups of Spanish-speaking people, including Cubans and Puerto Ricans. Coalitions of disenfranchised groups are also being developed.

Chicano involvement has seen a small rise in Chicano bureaucrats at the state and federal levels. Chicano bureaucrats work as agents between the established power structure and the general Chicano population. Though they risk becoming marginal to Chicano culture and to the dominant structure, they function to increase the communities' resources and upgrade their own standard of living.

During the 1960s and 1970s, it was not very difficult for Chicanos to find funding for projects addressing issues of housing, access to education, and employment. As a result, local leaders emerged and grant-proposal skills were developed. Some major national institutions, such as the National Council of La Raza, the Mexican American Legal Defense Foundation, and the National Association of Chicano

Studies, were created during the early period of activism. Their social activism and criticism continue.

Some community leaders pointed out that these large organizations had a chilling effect on local grass-roots activities. They took activities out of the control of grass-roots people. Grass-roots issues still include poverty, housing, and health care. These issues are subject to political manipulation. José Gutiérrez had a bitter conflict with Democratic candidate George McGovern, who accused him of having been neutral in the presidential election of 1972, in return for a $1 million health clinic given by the Republican administration to Crystal City. McGovern saw this trade-off as harmful to him. During his candidacy McGovern spoke positively about his support of Chicano concerns, but he lost the election and Chicano concerns suffered in the late 1970s.

In the 1980s, lack of mass nonelectoral politics has witnessed a decrease in institutionalized programs such as Chicano studies on college and university campuses. Bilingual education, which Chicanos acquired in the 1960s and the 1970s, was also losing funding and diminishing in mass political support. During the first five years of the Reagan administration, federal funding to states for job training programs declined by $27.8 billion (*Hispanic Link* 1986b). The membership of the U.S. Commission on Civil Rights was drastically reduced, and seven of its ten regional offices were closed. This eliminated civil rights staff that included Hispanics who had directed regional operations in New York and Texas for years. Because many programs had come to rely on the state and federal governments, the official policy to cut back on funding social service programs worked to undermine Chicano self-help activities.

THE NEXT GENERATION

In the 1980s the political language has changed. The press uses the label "Hispanic" rather than "Chicano" to refer to Mexican Americans. Hispanics no longer call themselves Chicanos. For some, the change in label is unacceptable. For others, the label Chicano is too radical (Blea 1984). Many also feel it is not inclusive of the various Spanish-speaking groups that exist in America. This all functions to fragment political efforts and has an impact on the next generation.

An issue of concern to contemporary and future leaders is the nature of the large number of Spanish-speaking immigrants, refugees, and undocumented workers. Mexican immigrants, despite their legal status in the United States, have the lowest naturalization rate. Thus, many of them do not have voting rights and are not politically active in either electoral or nonelectoral politics (De la Garza and Flores 1986).

Undocumented workers may be able to have some influence in labor unions, but their meager power will be interrupted by the immigration law of 1986. Chicanos have an interest in these new arrivals because they share not only their language but also their barrios and some of their history. Many Chicano citizens are related to these people, and there is a relatively high rate of intermarriage. Chicanos therefore involve themselves in undocumented workers' and immigrants' affairs.

The term "Hispanic" includes Chicanos, Mexicans, Puerto Ricans, Cubans, Central and Latin Americans, Europeans, and several island groups, plus other Spanish-speaking people. Unlike Chicanos and Puerto Ricans, Cubans tend to rally behind foreign-policy issues. The groups share an interest in bilingualism and social services. This tendency is likely to create more political power among active Hispanics. Hispanic coalitions are being enlarged. This group may merge its political minority activities with women, gays, the elderly, and the various poor people's movements. However, the larger the coalitions, the more difficult it is to maintain them because of varying interests.

In order to discuss strategies for the next generation, close observation of the political behavior of Hispanics is necessary. There is not always consensus. According to a survey conducted in 1981 and 1982 in East Los Angeles and in San Antonio, issues are not the same in all communities. The SVREP documented that Chicanos in San Antonio thought the most serious problem facing them was unemployment, and the Chicanos in East Los Angeles responded that crime was their most serious problem. When they were asked the most important problem facing the country, economic issues came to the top. Forty-five percent of the respondents in the two cities chose inflation as the most important problem, and 20 percent chose unemployment. The survey also indicates that the majority of Chicanos in the two cities think the U.S. government is spending too little money on domestic social issues such as education, Hispanic programs, bilingual education, halting crime, health, and drug abuse (De la Garza, Brischetto, and Vaughan 1983).

The SVREP survey also measured what affected the policy orientation of Chicanos. The use of mass media has little relationship to the forming of Chicano political opinion. The survey documented the importance of the informal network within Chicano communities. Spouse, family, and friends are most often involved in conversations about political or community issues. Eighty-three percent "never" talked with priests or ministers. Many Chicanos "never" talked with their bosses (79 percent) or civic organizational members (77 percent). When asked how important other individuals or organizations were in deciding how to vote, more than half of the respondents replied their spouse and relatives were "very important" or "somewhat important."

Membership in a political party and political participation rates are strongly related to educational attainment. The Chicano/Hispanic voter is not an exception. Sixty-three percent of the Hispanics who had been to college for four years or more, 54 percent of those with one to three years of college, 45 percent of high school graduates, and 37 percent with less than high school education cast their ballots in 1980 (Brischetto and Velásquez 1983). In general, professors, teachers, and managerial persons are more likely to vote than are laborers.

Another social reality is that those with higher incomes tend to be involved in politics more than do those with lower incomes. This also holds true for Chicanos. Employed Chicanos have higher political participation rates than the unemployed, and students are as interested in politics as the employed. These indicators can assist in developing political strategy, especially for the young adult.

Few organizations focus on Chicano youth as serious potential political leaders. This is because so much effort is necessary for activists just to maintain current involvements. The youth group constitutes a larger proportion of the total Chicano population than it does of the total Anglo population. Youths with a community base are certainly the directors of the Chicano future. Grass-roots activities at the community and state levels are just as important as activities at the national level. They might even be more important because of their immediate affect.

Chicanos are being more selective about whom they support. Being a Democrat and being Chicano may help obtain Chicano support, but it does not guarantee that support. Some people adhere to party loyalty. The SVREP's survey found that "Younger, more educated respondents are less likely to identify as Democrats than are older, less educated respondents" (*Businessweek* 1983, p. 17).

Leadership in the future may be divided into two types: the bureaucrat type and the community type. Both types will be important because they have both shaped the past and are the most tolerated by the establishment.

The bureaucrat types are the elected officials and executives in large organizations. These leaders attract mass media and have extensive networks. They are important because they represent Chicanos to Anglo America. If the leaders of this type succeed, Anglos will finally come to believe that Chicanos are able to do well in all spheres of life and will discard their antiquated racial biases. Chicano bureaucrats become role models for Chicano youth as well as for the Anglo. The bureaucratic leaders can spend more money and participate in the political process more easily, and are less threatening to the status quo.

Ironically, most of these leaders reject the label of Chicano. They are forced into this mode of behavior in order to gain acceptance. Denver mayor Federico Peña insisted throughout his campaign that he was not running as a Chicano candidate. He won with 51 percent of the vote even though Chicanos represent only about 18 percent of Denver's population and 12 percent of its registered voters. Henry G. Cisneros won with 94 percent of the vote in San Antonio, where Chicanos make up 54 percent of the population. The Cisneros and Peña strategy was not to alienate the Anglo vote.

A survey of nine politicians in the Denver metropolitan area reported that ethnicity was not a factor in their campaign because they themselves did not make it an issue (Perez 1983). Not making ethnicity an issue is an issue. Ethnicity is frequently an issue in the public as well as in the closed political circles.

Linda Chávez, who is of Spanish descent and was appointed to the U.S. Civil Rights Commission, is accused of having taken advantage of her ethnic background in order to gain her position while denouncing affirmative action for others (*Washington Monthly* 1985). Hispanic civil rights leaders were highly critical of her perceived inconsistency. The development of community leadership, especially that which gains national attention, is very important to grass-roots organizers. Although many Chicano leaders do not have effective influence outside of their communities, they have proven to be extremely effective where they live. Because of the Chicanos' interest in community issues and the fact that leaders arise from the community, the Chicanos maintain that all Chicano leaders are directly responsible to the people and should always work on behalf of the Chicano community.

The problems of Chicano communities vary in each area. Grass-roots activities led by people in these areas are the most effective vehicles to address community issues. Scholars and bureaucratic leaders recognize the importance of community at the grass-roots level.

Eight of the nine officials in the Denver metropolitan survey area answered "grass-roots strategy" when asked what they considered most important in their campaign (Perez 1983). The radical, critical Chicano leadership seen in the 1960s does not meet with the same acceptance today.

The general population and policymakers do not respond to marches, sit-ins, boycotts, and strikes. Radical strategy causes backlash. In fact, the overt conflicts between Chicanos/Hispanics and Anglos decreased when the movement became more moderate. Willie Velásquez of SVREP notes that Anglos in the Southwest are maturing. The SVREP receives fewer threatening letters and telephone calls.

Chicanos have taken an active role in educating racist Anglos, and some Anglos have responded. Chicanos have sensitized Anglos in their own self-interest. To some it is unacceptable that Chicanos must struggle within the existing system in order to change it.

SUMMARY

Prior to the 1970s Chicano efforts to address their social condition were mainly based on nonelectoral activities. Although there were some Chicano politicians before the Chicano movement, these men (women were very few) did not always represent the interests of Chicanos. They sometimes supported the Anglo in order to avoid conflicts or to maintain their status. Under the circumstances, Chicanos could not access the political process as a means by which to address their issues, and attention was given to education, to the labor movement, and, to a limited extent, the judicial system and discrimination during the "zoot suit" trials in California.

The United States is not a melting pot for Chicanos. The assimilation model does not work for them and does not account for their experiences. During the Chicano movement, the internal colonial model evolved as a means to explain the Chicano experience. This model, and the decolonization aspect of it, have motivated Chicanos in academe and politics since the 1960s.

The Chicano movement in the 1960s may be understood as a force that identified and exposed the internal colonial system. Chicanos attracted national attention and created national awareness. These efforts were directly and indirectly supported by other movements. The Anglo hippie movement was criticizing American culture. The Vietnam War protesters criticized foreign policy. The black civil rights movement, the American Indian movement, and the women's movement all fueled Chicano activities, and Chicano activities fueled other critical efforts. During this time Chicanas openly discussed poverty, housing, social services, Chicanismo, racism, police brutality, murals, theater, poetry, union organizing, education, bilingualism, project funding, sexism, the role of the Catholic Church, upward mobility, youth, the family, and politics. Through these efforts, substantial gains were made.

In the late 1970s and early 1980s, these gains were lessened or lost. The general situation for the average person of color in the United States grew worse. Chicanos appear to have failed to decolonize themselves, but the efforts have not been abandoned. The Chicano movement produced the internal colonial model and participation in electoral politics. The U.S. government and its people were forced to listen to the demands of Chicanos, and the Chicano people supported one another. Even after nonelectoral activities were diminished, the number of Chicano officials rose and the movement proceeded as a reform movement. In this context, then, the decolonization of the Chicano continues. Decolonization efforts manifest themselves as Chicanos practicing law and as business persons. There are 250,000 Hispanic-owned firms in the country. They earned about $15 billion in sales and receipts in 1982, and tend to be small and family operated. In 1988 their generated revenue was expected to be $98 billion.

Some factors to consider in discussing the Chicano future include mobilization and political education of Chicano youth, the enlargement of grass-roots populations and grass-roots activities, the demise of unions and federal-state funding, and the importance of women and leadership development.

REFERENCES

Acuna, Rodolfo. 1981. *Occupied America: A History of Chicanos*, p. 361. New York: Harper and Row.

Blea, Irene I. 1984. "Social Political Strategies for the Next Generation." Paper presented at the National Association for Chicano Studies, Sacramento, CA.

Brischetto, Robert R., and Willie Velásquez. 1983. *The Hispanic Electorates*, pp. 139–47. San Antonio: Southwest Voter Registration Education Project.

Businessweek. 1983. "Hispanic Power Arrives at the Ballot Box." July 4, p. 17.

De la Garza, Rodolfo O., and Robert Brischetto, with David Vaughan. 1983. *The Mexican American Electorate: Information Sources and Policy Orientations*, pp. 6–12. Occasional Paper no. 2. Austin, TX: Southwest Voter Registration Education Project and HPSP of the Center of Mexican American Studies.

De la Garza, Rodolfo O., and Adela Flores. 1986. "The Impact of Mexican Immigrants: Clarification of Issues and Some Hypotheses for Future Research." In Harley L. Browning and Rodolfo de la Garza, eds., *Mexican Immigrants and Mexican Americans: An Evolving Relation*, pp. 211–26. Austin, TX: CMAS Publications.

García, F. Chris, and Rodolfo de la Garza. 1977. *The Chicano Political Experience: Three Perspectives*, pp. 79, 97–116. North Scituate, MA: Duxbury Press.

Hispanic Link Weekly Report. 1986a. 4, no. 38 (September 22): p. 1.

———. 1986b. 4, no. 40 (October 6): 1, 3.

———. 1986c. 4, no. 46 (November 17): 1.

Martínez, Arthur. 1979. *Who's Who of Chicano Office Holders*. 2nd ed. Silver City, NM: author.

———. 1987. *Who's Who*. . . . 6th ed., pp. 6–7. Silver City, NM: author.

Morgan, Thomas B. 1983. "The Latinization of America." *Esquire*, May, p. 54.

Newsweek. 1983. "Hispanic Power at the Polls." July 4, p. 28.

New York Times. 1984. "The New York Times/CBS News Poll." November 8, p. 83.

Nuestro. 1984. "Women, Power and the Vote." 16: 43–44.

Perez, Magdalena. 1983. "Campaign Strategies of Chicano/Hispano Elected Officials." In Irene I. Blea, ed., Chicano Studies Political Participation Project, pp. 11–13, 26.

Rocky Mountain News. 1986. "Hispanics Get Out the Vote." September 19, pp. 6, 13.

Thernstrom, Stephan, ed. 1980. *Harvard Encyclopedia of American Ethnic Groups*, p. 71. Cambridge, MA: Belknap Press.

U.S.A. Today. 1985. "Hispanics Test Political Clout at Polls." November 5, pp. 1A–2A.

U.S. Bureau of the Census. 1984. *Condition of Hispanics in America Today.* Washington, D.C.: U.S. Government Printing Office, p. 31.

U.S. News & World Report. 1983. "The Disappearing Border." August 22, p. 48.

Velásquez, Willie. 1986. "Electoral Politics and the Chicano Voter." Speech delivered to the Chicano Caucus, Denver, March 6.

Washington Monthly. 1985. "Just One of the Guys: Linda Chavez and the Exploitation of Ethnic Identity." (June): pp. 34–39.

Washington Post. 1986. "Washington Gains Support in Chicago Wards." April 30, p. A–3.

7
Toward a Renewed Social Science

INTRODUCTION

Knowledge of Chicano history, and of the issues of language and culture, have given many Mexican Americans a Third World perspective. This viewpoint is highly critical of the United States and its policies. The Third World perspective fundamentally goes like this: The United States acted as an imperialist country in its violent strategy to obtain and retain the northern Mexican territory. It imposed an internal colonial structure on the newly conquered people as a means of social control.

Violence, force, and discrimination have been used to bar the Chicano from upward and outward mobility. The Mexican American has been dispossessed of land and other resources, and remains powerless. Education, politics, low health standards, and poverty have been vehicles of social oppression. Similar vehicles have been used to suppress other countries, especially underdeveloped countries. This historical and ideological construct links the Chicano to international affairs and explains why Chicanos are sensitive to Third World issues. They have been victimized by comparable U.S. tactics since the early 1800s, and large numbers of them have held this perspective since the 1960s. A theoretical approach to the study of Mexican Americans must clearly recognize this viewpoint. It is also a point of view that is a direct contribution to the development of the social sciences.

ACKNOWLEDGING THE CONTRIBUTION

Thus far, sociology has evolved as the study of society focusing upon the social institutions and how they function to create, sustain, and change society. It has influenced other sciences. This approach to the study of American human organization has incorporated a micro-macro perspective and has progressed mostly upon the view of society as somewhat static and generally not changing radically.

For Anglo Americans perhaps this is true. Social change is relative to one's social condition. A minority group, however, is subject to more intense and more frequent social change than are other populations. This flux is directly linked to power: the less power, the more change. This has a special effect on minority women, who have even less social power than minority men. For minority people, historical events have severely impacted their social reality to the extent that their daily placement in society, their attitudes and behaviors, are affected.

To continue to function in the social sciences as if these facts do not exist is to engage in self-deception and to stunt the growth of knowledge. This would be an international disgrace because advances in ethnic studies, especially Chicano studies and women's studies, are the newest developments in academe and are an American production. It is incumbent upon American social scientists to take responsibility for their study of social reality by grounding it in reality and extending it to the rest of the world.

The first step in updating American social science is to recognize the Chicano and other minority experiences as a social experience primarily forced upon people. This would advance the study of social control. Emphasis must be placed upon the fact that a social-historical approach is in order. American society as a whole is characterized by stability, uneven development, and very slow social change.

Chicano scholars have contributed greatly to the recognition that some Americans are not immigrants and have become Americans under the adverse conditions of force, war, conquest, and violence. American social scientists can make a grand contribution to knowledge and peace by acknowledging the existence of this terribly dehumanizing occurrence and the fact that it continues in some highly sophisticated ways. This is a social phenomenon that is characterized by discrimination, social oppression, and projection of blame onto the victim. The study of social oppression can be expanded as an area of specialization. This area of specialization is different from, and encompasses, race relations and gender studies that address discriminating social factors. In sociology, scholars working in the area rarely use a social-historical model.

The study of the oppressive nature of social institutions must emphasize ideology as an element of social control. Social discrimination must be raised from its current latent place in sociology and made manifest as the strong social force that it is. It characterizes people's daily life through every other social institution. Social oppression is more than an institution. It is like a veil that hovers above and laces throughout the fabric of society.

The manifestation of social-historical oppression as an area of concentration, an area of priority, would assist the contemporary social scientist in value clarification. Important in this endeavor is the politics of research and the social sciences. As a young scholar I frequently asked myself, "Why do social science?" Aside from the naive answer that I liked it, that it interested me, I rationally concluded that one "does" social science as a means by which to understand society and the world, and in order to apply these findings, these understandings, and make the society a better place to live. As a middle-aged scholar I still believe this, even though I know some academics do social science because it pays their household expenses.

The investigation of social-historical oppression should recognize the internal colonial model as well as the academic contribution of racial and ethnic minorities. As academe is now constructed, these contributions are limited to a marginal presence in the teaching of race relations and gender studies, primarily in ethnic and women's studies programs. They need to be integrated.

THE INTERNAL COLONIAL MODEL REVIEWED

The internal colonial model has been presented as the dominant theoretical perspective lending insight to the Chicano experience. It is a social-historical model that focuses upon institutional racism as a social fact that systematically discriminates against and controls Chicanos by keeping them at the lower socioeconomic level for generations. Elements of the internal colonial model not yet fully discussed are the concepts of decolonization and feminism, and their relationship. Decolonization calls for the elimination of colonization, the deposing of oppression. At its extreme, decolonization calls for armed revolt. At a more mild level it calls for institutional reform. It has been a feminist assumption that this perspective has included women and inherently calls for feminist, egalitarian action.

In the 1960s armed revolt was a serious consideration adopted by members of the Brown Berets and others. Over the years this option has quieted, and reform of social institutions has taken precedence. Social reform for the Chicano has taken the route that most oppressed people have taken in other parts of the world. It began with consciousness: class, race, and gender consciousness during an era of extreme social criticism in America. In the 1960s, through Lyndon B. Johnson's War on Poverty, ethnic and racial minorities became more aware that it is people of color who are poor in America. This led to a self-acceptance movement among minorities and women. "Black Is Beautiful" became a black national assertion. Prior to this, black was not considered beautiful, even by blacks. Patterned after the "Black Is Beautiful" campaign, Chicanos stated that "Brown Is Beautiful." They defiantly adopted the label "Chicano" as a means of identification.

The American capitalist system needs Chicanos. It needs the poor. Their adverse social position and poverty serve as constant reminders that conformity is expected. At the same time that racial-ethnic minority people serve as role models of what will happen if conformity does not take place, they also act as a reserve army of labor when they are not employed and as a cheap labor force when some of them are employed. A fundamental assumption of this mental construction is that Chicanos and Chicano culture can have value for the dominant culture only when they produce profit and when they are removed from a critical ideology. Knowing this angers Chicanos and makes them resistant. This is natural human anger produced over time and is rooted in frustration, violence, and oppression.

That Chicanos resist assimilation into a social system that punishes them is a well-known fact. This system has attempted to erase Chicanos from consideration. It has erased their history, and their literary and artistic contributions, and has acted to suppress this production by degrading and suppressing the Chicanos or ignoring them altogether. If anything has survived, it has been because of Chicano resistance, preservation, and conscious production.

Chicanos go further than criticizing the system; they criticize themselves. It is part of their culture to enter into self-criticism. Though they do not know who their philosophers might have been, they know that their own social and historical actions can produce behaviors that sometimes are self-defeating. The earliest cultural variable open to self-criticism was machismo. Women opened the discussion and recorded that machismo had changed in meaning. It was once a term that connoted self-pride, self-respect, respect for others, and masculine honor. However, its use in the English language has changed it to mean stubborn, ruthless, and endowed with delusions of sexual grandeur. Because of interaction with the dominant society, machismo became a sexist-racist stereotype.

Interaction with dominant America has also led Mexican American women to internalize sexist attitudes. Mexican American women give insight into assimilation when they discuss attempting to meet the dominant American standard. They focus upon the "admission price" into the white-male-dominated world. The price is manifested in a thing not often recognized by dominant Americans: the suppression and violation of the spirit. Basically, too much assimilation is bad for Chicanos. Their spirit dies. They lose the thing that links them to nature, the thing that links them to others.

Chicanos have demanded and brought about some changes in education, politics, employment, social welfare policies, and their personal lives, but they have failed to politicize the next generation. Their energies have been consumed by the heavy burdens of keeping society "straight," maintaining households and dependents. Some of them have raised their income. They are no longer in poverty, and their children have not grown up in barrios. They have taught their children how to "make it" in the system, and they have evidence that they have succeeded. However, many complain that their children want little more than upward mobility, good jobs, and more money.

Civil rights movement people sometimes worry about those who did not "make it" at the same time they are thankful that they themselves did. Because of their sense of community, they sometimes feel guilty for having "made it." Yet some abandon the ethnic movement and the barrio once they have economic security. Others continue to work on behalf of extended family and relatives. Very many still spend their time, energy, and money on resocializing white America to Chicano ways and in socializing Chicanos to white American ways. They organize fund raisers, marches, scholarships, and receptions to honor their own members and to raise funds to continue operation. As a whole, they have a multifaceted approach to decolonization. One can find them at every level in society, but all too frequently they are few.

THE POLITICS OF SOCIAL SCIENCE

Since the 1960s the social sciences have had a political use. Social science research was used to legitimize funding in the social services and to gain an understanding of the civil discontent that plagued the country. The social sciences have established certain social facts. Emile Durkheim contended that, given certain social conditions, a social phenomenon would arise. Social forces emanate from group lifestyles. This radiation is not ambivalent. In the case of minorities in society, it directs discriminatory behavior, class bigotry, racism, and sexism. Discrimination is a social fact.

Durkheim (1966) emphasized that social facts are general throughout society. Social facts are truths about the nature of society. By this he did not mean that facts exist without exception, but that they could potentially be universal. He contends that if certain social conditions exist, a social phenomenon will arise anywhere. A second criterion defining a social fact is that it is a social force exercising power and control over individuals. The existence of a social fact is evidenced by the consequences, the impact, that its existence has on individuals. American sociologists, like some of those of other countries, have followed the thinking of Durkheim without noting that he was interested not in developing sociology as a science but in developing the sociological method (Solovay et al. 1966, p. 8). Durkheim was interested in using an approach that provided a new instrument that all social sciences could use in their studies. In doing this, social facts were extremely important to him. His focus was upon the possibility of the social sciences and the psychological sciences. His second interest was in the existence of social facts and their possible use to expand this possibility.

American social scientists have proceeded in their science as if social facts were general, universal, without consideration of cultural manifestations and their political use. Early work on Mexican Americans conducted by Anglo social scientists was inaccurate and laden with biases because they assumed that what was true in their own culture was true in other cultures. They continued their analysis, assuming that their cultural reality was the standard and the appropriate reality, and that all else was incorrect or somehow inferior. The political manifestations of using the social sciences in this way have severely limited the life chances of Chicanos and other minorities.

We have seen the creation and reaction of social victims. Given the American condition, what has happened to racial-ethnic minorities was bound to happen. The proof that society created these conditions exists both within and outside the U.S. national boundaries. A Third World perspective in the Chicano community evolved because social oppression existed. It continues because social oppression continues. When a society is thus characterized, it sets up conditions for social revolution. This, however, is not the political stance of racial-ethnic minorities and women. They desire social reform, the realignment of conditions in order to allow them to participate.

REALIGNING THE SOCIAL SCIENCES

The American experience is unique but not isolated. Oppressed countries have developed the same critical perspective in isolation from their American counterpart. Consistent with Durkheim's contention, given certain circumstances of social-historical imperialistic tactics (conquest, force, and violence), a society (a government) will experience extreme resistance by those populations it wants to force into its society at a substandard level.

People need power and control over their own lives. It is especially expected in a competitive culture. Resistance becomes a social force exercising power and control. Breaking the dominant, established norms is resistance. Negative consequences reaffirm the need of the oppressed to resist.

For those who feel social scientists have a social resposibility to apply their findings, the question of what to do with the politics of social science becomes immediate. The answer is simple: stop it. Stop making the social sciences a political tool to reaffirm the status quo. The social sciences can assist white America by taking a position against the political use of social science and truly engaging in it as a science. Social scientists must stop being threatened and masking their insecurities. They must allow racial-ethnic minority people to be themselves without an attached scientific opinion. They can no longer escape responsibility by skirting reality and arguing that no one is to blame. We are to blame.

In order to move the social sciences from their present stalemate, I suggest an evaluation of their fundamental premises, a review of their objectives, and a decision of purpose. I further suggest a critique of the language used in conducting social science. Words laden with value connotations should be stripped from social science language. This act in itself would go far in removing the inherent discrimination exhibited in a hierarchically structured culture and would raise American social science to an international level of recognition.

Most of my concerns on the nature of social science and research are not new. Scholars have taken opinions on many sides of these issues. I feel the rejuvenation of the questions is important, for it gives direction for value clarification for both younger and older scholars. After all, social scientists have power, status, and prestige. They cannot escape the fact that other members of society defer to the opinions of the experts. Americans look to them for guidance. This is why ethnic-racial minorities, poor people, and women need so desperately to influence their thinking and behaviors. This is why Chicano studies has been so very important in the battle of ideas.

REVIEWING THE DISCRIMINATION CYCLE

A final brief definition of discrimination and how it functions is in order. Discrimination is defined as social action, both intentional and unintentional, that creates and sustains a dominant-subordinate relationship that ensures privilege for members of the dominant society. Discrimination places restrictions on the oppressed group. It limits their activities and their opportunities. Laws and other policies are applied selectively. Intergroup contact is restricted. The oppressed group is subject to more physical and psychological violence. It is omitted from planning, which creates conflict at both overt and latent levels. It is a phenomenon that supports the giving of economic and political advantage to a select few. This power, however, does not go unquestioned. Ethnic and racial minorities question power relationships, and they have taken action to address them.

Racism is a doctrine, an attitude. Some members of society do not recognize racism because they have blind spots. They may not want to see it, recognize it, and take responsibility for it. If they choose not to see racism, it may be because racism is violent and nasty, dehumanizing and evil. Not seeing it is a protective mechanism.

Racism is a pervasive phenomenon for both the racist and the victim. If individuals are subjected to continued racism, they will internalize it and base much of their behavior upon racist messages.

Major social institutions, such as the family, the church, and the educational system, have racism built into them. They help maintain the status quo through the socialization process, by which people learn culture. Individuals learn culture from the people who comprise society. This constructs what is valued as normal behavior. To a great degree, the circumstances of one's birth are attributed to chance.

Today Chicanos live in two cultures, and discrimination affects the individual both personally and socially. Chicanos are born into two cultures. One of these cultures is in an adversary power relationship to the other. Because of racism, Chicanos have little interaction with white culture, but they are expected to function in it. At the time of a child's birth, the parents have been subjected to discrimination. The parents and other Chicanos in the family, in the community, have learned some coping skills. The child will be subjected to those skills and messages before reaching school age.

Chicanos talk about racism in their homes, at parties, at work. The fact that Chicanos traditionally do not leave the barrio gives the child the message that he/she belongs there, and few other places. Sometimes parents are uneasy being with white people. The child picks up this feeling. Perhaps the owner of the neighborhood grocery store is white. Perhaps the manager of the gas station, the fireman, the policeman, the priest is white. The child learns that people in positions of authority, with incomes, are white even before going to school, where the teachers and the principal are white. Perhaps the janitor is Chicano or black or Vietnamese, or the child knows a few unemployed Chicano persons. Perhaps the best the child can hope to be is a janitor, a clerk at the grocery store, a gas station attendant. Often the child wants to be a policeman, or a priest, or a teacher. The child finds out that priests are expected to practice celibacy, and changes his mind. When the police are recognized as always watching Chicanos, children stop wanting to be a policeman.

The average white child, on the other hand, has a different experience. This child learns that racism exists but he or she is immune to it. As a small child the Anglo hears "Mexican" jokes. Thus, Mexicans are related to humor and inferiority. Most of the racist jokes are about Mexicans being lazy, stupid, or late. Thus, the child assumes that this is how they are. Or a white child's early experience with Mexicans may be in the context of music, dancing, singing, or a vacation. The child learns that Mexicans, and Mexican culture, are for entertainment only. It is not a viable aspect of the child's life.

This child does not receive a message that conveys positive, competent images.

The use of language is important to children. They learn about the structure of the society through how language is used. The white child who is unfortunate enough not to encounter Chicanos early in life at least learns that blacks exist. The colors black and white become important. White has connotations of being positive and black of being negative: white magic and black magic, the fairy princess dressed in white and the wicked witch, in black, and bad things happening at night, in the dark, while it is safer by day, in the light. All children hear and use the English language and receive its messages. The white child learns he or she is superior, and grows up acting this way. The Chicano child feels brown is closer to black.

Much psychological violence is performed in the field of education. Up to school age children trust adults. This gives adults the power to brainwash them. As has been stated, parents are also victims of brainwashing. It is sad and frustrating that, in spite of all documentation, teachers still teach that Columbus discovered America, that the Pilgrims were the first white settlers, and that America was the "New World." Teachers refuse to recognize that America was not discovered. It already existed and was inhabited by people representing grand and ancient civilizations. The Pilgrims were not the first white settlers.

At one level nobody is to blame for racism. It is inherited. At another level, all of society is to blame as long as racism is allowed to continue. A fundamental contention is that humans are, by their nature, social beings. As social beings they fall into groups. Because they have relationships, they have a responsibility to one another. Because American cultural values stress individualism, many claim that this is not true. This keeps the society from social advancement. There is no such thing as inaction. A lack of action is a decision, and it carries social responsibility.

Social responsibility affects even the classroom. Frustration begins early and is relentless. Chicano youth do not drop out of school, they are pushed out. Their "push out," however, is not a total failure. Chicano children have had degradation and devaluation drilled into their heads. They learn that whites discovered and built the United States; that they are conquerors, the biggest, the best, the most powerful, the most intelligent; and that only they can lead. Some come to doubt the messages. They sit in classrooms with secret questions, secret insights, secret conclusions, and they finally drop out when they can no longer tolerate the pain.

Many stop trying. They cannot conform to the lies, to the oppressive structure. Placing artificial value on lies, things that are unimportant, uninteresting, and totally irrelevant, is recognized as a waste of time. A typical "push out" is really very sophisticated. He/she needs to retain the cultural value that distinguishes between Anglos and Chicanos: the combination of personal dignity and respect. Once respect is lost, it cannot be regained. Hispanics give respect to all who are born. They resist taking it away. Respect is more fluid in Anglo culture than it is in Chicano culture. In Chicano culture it is ascribed at birth; in Anglo culture it is an achieved status.

One reason both young men and women give for dropping out of school is pregnancy. Men leave to support and women leave to raise a family. When this occurs, the Chicano youth has attempted three things: (1) to demonstrate that he or she has not failed; (2) to retain respect because he or she has taken responsibility for an action; and (3) to achieve adult status by becoming a parent. In reality, dropping out of school is a survival tactic. It is an escape from the humiliation, the pain, the anguish of the educational process. Although it keeps the youth culturally intact, it sets up a cycle of poverty and more social punishment.

SUMMARY

What has been discussed in this book influences everyone. All members of society play a role in sustaining discrimination, dissolving it, or changing it. Chicano activists feel it is impossible not to take an action. If societal members only work and pay bills and mind their own business, they are not socially involved. They are involved at a purely individual level. Many Americans tend to think and act this way. Activists feel that if they are not part of the solution, they are part of the problem. And discrimination is a social problem.

Some activists feel that not only Anglos have to change. Many Chicanos also have to change. They must learn that there are some very fine white people and other people of color who are not racist and/or sexist. They must learn to trust these people and to work with them toward a better society. Activists contend that Chicanos need to rid themselves of all internalized messages and acceptance of inferiority, insecurity, and hostility. They must assert their power and continue taking responsibility for their people, their society. They must claim America as theirs and not feel they are abandoning or deserting their past.

REFERENCE

Durkheim, Emile. 1966. *The Rules of Sociological Method.* 8th ed. Translated by Sarah A. Solovay and John H. Mueller, edited by George E. G. Catlin. New York: Free Press. Original work entitled *Les regles de la méthode sociologique* (1895).

Selected Bibliography

Acuna, Rodolfo. 1972. *Occupied America: The Struggle Toward Chicano Liberation*. San Francisco: Canfield.

———. 1981. *Occupied America: A History of Chicanos*. San Francisco: Harper and Row. 2nd ed. of *Occupied America* (1972).

Baca-Zinn, Maxine, Lynn Cannon, Elizabeth Higgenbotham, and Bonnie Thorton Dill. 1986. "The Costs of Exclusionary Practices in Women's Studies." *Signs: Journal of Women in Culture and Society* 2, no. 21: 290–303.

Barrera, Mario. 1979. *Race and Class in the Southwest*. South Bend, IN: Notre Dame University Press.

Becker, Howard S. 1963. *Outsiders: Studies in the Sociology of Deviance*. New York: Free Press.

Blalock, Hubert M., Jr. 1967. *Toward a Theory of Minority Group Relations*. New York: Capricorn Books.

Blauner, Robert. 1969. "Internal Colonialism and Ghetto Revolt." *Social Problems* 16 (Spring):393–408.

———. 1972. *Racial Oppression in America*. New York: Harper and Row.

Blea, Irene. 1980. "Bessemer: A Sociological Perspective of a Chicano Barrio." Ph.D. diss., University of Colorado, Boulder.

———. 1988. *Bessemer: A Sociological Perspective of a Chicano Barrio*. New York: AMS Press.

Burkey, Richard. 1978. *Ethnic and Racial Groups: The Dynamics of Dominance*. Menlo Park, CA: Benjamin/Cummings.

Camarillo, Alberto. 1979. *Chicanos in a Changing Society*. Cambridge, MA: Harvard University Press.

Cervantes, Fred A. 1973. "Chicanos as a Post-Colonial Minority: Some Questions Concerning the Adequacy of the Paradigm of Internal Colonialism." *Perspectives in Chicano Studies*. Los Angeles: Chicano Studies Publications.

Cordova, Theresa, Norma Cantu, Gilberto Cardenas, Juan García, and Christine M. Sierra. 1986. *Chicana Voices: Intersections of Class, Race and Gender*. Austin: University of Texas, CMAS Publications.

Durkheim, Emile. 1915. *The Elementary Forms of the Religious Life*. London: George Allen and Unwin.

———. 1966a. *Suicide*, J. Spaulding and George Simpson, trans. New York: Free Press. Original work published 1897.

———. 1966b. *The Rules of Sociological Method*. 8th ed. Translated by Sarah A. Solovay and John H. Mueller, edited by George E. G. Catlin. New York: Free Press. Original work, *Les regles de la méthode sociologique*, published in 1895.

Fanon, Frantz. 1963. *The Wretched of the Earth*. New York: Grove Press.

Firestone, Shulamith. 1972. *The Dialectic of Sex*. New York: Bantam Books.

García, F. Chris, and Rodolfo de la Garza. 1977. *The Chicano Political Experience: Three Perspectives*. North Scituate, MA: Duxberry Press.

Gelford, Donald E. 1982. *Aging: The Ethnic Factor*. Boston: Little Brown.

Gilfix, Michael. 1977. "A Case of Unequal Suffering." *Generations* 3 (Summer): pp. 8–11.

Griswold del Castillo, Richard. 1984. *La Familia: Chicano Families in the Urban Southwest, 1848 to the Present*. South Bend, IN: University of Notre Dame Press.

Goffman, Erving. 1961. *Asylum*. Chicago: Aldine.

Hirschi, Travis. 1969. *Causes of Delinquency*. Berkeley: University of California Press.

Juaquez, Rolando A. 1976. "What the Tape Recorder Has Created: A Broadly Based Exploration into Contemporary Oral History Practice." *Aztlan: International Journal of Chicano Studies* (Spring): pp. 22–26.

Keller, Gary D. 1985. *Chicano Cinema: Research, Reviews, and Resources*. Binghamton, NY: Bilingual Review Press.

Krohn, Marvin D., and James L. Massey. 1980a. "Social Control and Delinquent Behavior: An Examination of the Social Bond." *Sociological Quarterly* 21 (Autumn):529–43.

———. 1980b. "Social Status and Deviance." *Criminology* 18: 303–18.

Mead, George Herbert. 1934. *Mind, Self and Society: The Standpoint of a Behaviorist*, Charles W. Morris, ed. Chicago: University of Chicago Press.

Melville, Margaritta B. 1980. *Twice a Minority*. St. Louis: C. V. Mosby.

Memmi, Albert. 1965. *The Colonizer and the Colonized*. Boston: Beacon Press.

Merton, Robert K. 1957. *Social Theory and Social Structure*. New York: Free Press.

Mirande, Alfred. 1985. *The Chicano Experience*. South Bend, IN: University of Notre Dame Press.

Mirande, Alfredo, and Evangelina Enríquez. 1979. *La Chicana*. Chicago: University of Chicago Press.

Moore, Joan W., Robert García, Carlos García, Luis Cerda, and Frank Valencia. 1979. *Homeboys: Gangs, Drugs and Prison in the Barrios of Los Angeles*. Philadelphia: Temple University Press.

Myrdal, Gunnar. 1944. *American Dilemma*. New York: Harper.

Newquist, Deborah. 1977. "Aging Across Cultures." *Generations* 3 (Summer):17–23.

Norwood, Robin. 1985. *Women Who Love too Much*. New York: Simon and Schuster.

Nye, F. Ivan. 1958. *Family Relationships and Delinquent Behavior*. New York: Wiley.

Paredes, Américo. 1958. *With a Pistol in His Hand: A Border Ballad and Its Hero*. Austin: University of Texas Press.

Reckless, Walter C. 1973. *The Crime Problem*. 5th ed. New York: Appleton-Century-Crofts.

Rocky Mountain News. 1979. Denver, CO, May 6.

Scamehorn, H. Lee. 1966. *Pioneer of the West*. Boulder, CO: Pruett.

Sutherland, Edwin H. 1961. *White Collar Crime*. New York: Holt, Rinehart and Winston.

Valle, Ramón. 1977. "Natural Networks: Paths to Service." *Generations* 3 (Summer):36–41.

Warner, W. Lloyd, and Leo Srole. 1945. *The Social Systems of American Ethnic Groups*. New Haven: Yale University Press.

Wiatrowski, Michael D., David B. Griswold, and Mary K. Roberts. 1981. "Social Control Theory and Delinquency." *American Sociological Review* 46 (October):525–41.

Index

academe, and race relation, women, and Chicano Studies, 36–37
accommodation, 10
acculturation, 10
Acuna, Rudolpho, 2, 14, 20, 23, 112
addiction, 52, 65
Alamo, and Davey Crockett, Jim Bowie, 109
American Democratic Organization, 10
American dream, and men, women, and the working class, 32–33
Anaya, Tony, 128
Arizona, 24, 101; politics of, 121, 128
art, 96
assimilation, 10, 11–14, 35, 134–35, 142–43
Aztec women, and childbirth, 73

"baby boom," 62
Baca, Felipe (Colorado Territorial Legislator), 101
Baca, Polly (Colorado State Senator), 101
Baca-Zinn, Maxine, 82
baptismo, 49

Barrera, Mario, 84, 100–105, 106
barrio, 65; creation, economics, politics, 4, 100
biculturalism, and Chicanos, 30
bilingualism: and biculturalism, 35; in education, 130
birth control, and abortion, 71
black Americans, 5–7, 13–14, 147; children, 147; community studies, 4; discrimination, 83, 96; education, 14; ghetto, 100; immigration, 14; internal colonial model, 19; and language, use of, 148; males, 42; organizations, 10; poverty, 30–31; and research, 63; slavery, 20; women, 39
black civil rights movement, 70, 118, 135
Black Is Beautiful, 244
black organizations, 11
black people, in Mexico, 23
black studies, 109
black women, in the civil rights movement, 70–71
"blaming the victim," 8; academic per-

spective, 14; Ryan William, 14; women, 51–52
Blauner, Robert, 102
Blea, Irene, 71, 82
Bracero Program, World War II, 117
Brown, Beret, 142
brujeria, 49
bureaucrat, Chicano, 133
business, entrepreneurship, 135

California, 24, 101, 121; politics, 121, 128
Camarillo, 100
capitalism, and discrimination, 142
caste, and class, race, and gender, 30
Catholicism, and importance of religion, 63–64
Chávez, Cesar, 120
Chávez, Linda, 133
Chicanas, and feminism, 67–89
Chicanismo, 97
Chicano movement, 118–21
Chicano studies, 109
Cholos, 106
Christianity, 197
Christmas, 56–57
class, lower, middle, and upper, 30
Colorado, politics, 121, 128
Commission on Civil Rights, United States, 131
compadres (godparents), 50
competition, 145
confirmation, 49
Cortez, Gregorio, 110
Cortez, Hernan, 74–75
Cortinas, Cheno, 110
Cotera, Martha, 73, 82
criminal justice system, dual standard of, 96
Crusade for Justice, 10, 119
Crystal City, 130
Cubans, politics and, 129
culture, 47–48
curanderismo, 49
Cycle of poverty, of Gunner Myrdal, 83–84

death rate of Chicanos, Chicanas, and Anglos, 42

decolonization, 103–8, 135; resistence, 106
democracy, 95
Democratic candidate, 130
Democratic Party, 117, 121, 122, 115–135
Democrats, 122–24, 132; New Mexico, congressmen, 128
deportation, the role of women in, 80
deviance theory, and stratifiction, 31–32
deviants, 92–97
Diaz del Castillo, 75
discrimination, multifaceted cycle of, 86
doctors, 108
"drop outs," ("push outs"), 148–49

Easter, Penitenes and, 56
economics, 106
Education, psychological violence and, 139
elderly, 47, 59–63, 64, 108; study of (gerontology), 59–64
El Partido de La Raza Unida, 10
Espinoza brothers, 110
ethnicity, 59–63, 108

family, American dream, 64; black, female headed, 17; "Corky" Gonzales, 118–19; extended, 63–64, 143; gatherings, 91; information system, 60; involvement in politics, 119, 132, 135; liberation theology, and the church, 58; racism, 69; religion, 110, 135; small business, 134; socialization, 146; Spanish language, 106; value structure, 97, 124
Fanon, Frantz, 102
Firestone, Shulamith, 83
Florida, 121
Food Stamp Program, social workers and, 37
funerals, role of women and children, 55

G. I. Forum, 117
Garcia, Chris, 105, 118, 126

Garcia, Hector, 117; and the G. I.
Forum, 117
Garcia, Mario, 45
Garcia, Robert, 117; and the Demo-
cratic Party, 127
gender roles, socialization of men and
women in Chicano culture and, 39
gerrymandering, 128
ghosts, 49
Godparents (madrina, padrino, com-
padres, comadre), 50
Goffman, Erving, 100
Gonzales, Rodolfo "Corky," 118–19
government, U.S. and poverty and
Chicanos in the 1960s, 32
Gutierrez, Jose Angel, 119

health, 139
Hermanos Penitentes, 56
Hernandez-Tovar, Inez, 82
high school graduates, 132
Hispanics (Chicanos, Mexicans, Puerto
Ricans, and Cubans), 131; Hispanic
vote, and media attention, 115

ideology, 32, 35, 58, 102, 110; community, 30; of liberation, 32; and religion, 58
Illinois, politics of, 121
immigration, 15, 21, 120, 131; undocumented workers, 131
Indian culture, 49
Indian indigenous people, 97. *See also*
Native Americans
intermarriage, 50–51
internal colonial model, 100, 141; feminism and, 72

Jesus Christ, 147
jokes, Mexican, racist, sexist, 147
Juaquez, Rolando, 103

Kansas, politics of, 126
Keller, Gary, 8

La Alianza: land grants, 119–20; National Forest campgrounds, 119–20

La Alianza Federal de Mercedes, 10,
120
labor: cheap, 14, 32, 37; division of,
22; hard labor, capitalist workers,
32; slavery, 15; women, 30–32, 39,
71–72
La Llorona (Malintzin, Dona Marina,
La Malinchi), 74–75
land, 15, 20–22, 30, 50, 100; displacement, 80, 120, 139; indigenous
groups, 100; Mexican Revolution
and women, 79; spirituality and, 77
land grants, 23, 80, 120; Alienza Federal de Mercedes, 120; law suits, 79;
Reis Lopes Tijerina, 119–20
language(s), 97, 108; and children, and
Mexicans, 148; English and Spanish,
110
La Raza Unida, 119
La Raza Unida Party, 71, 119–20
Las Gorras Blancas, 10, 110
lateral thinking, women, survival, and,
86–87
law, 110, 135
League of United Latin American Citizens (LULAC), 116
leadership, youth and, 133
liberation, 55
liberation theology, 58
life expectancy, 42
literature, 96
Los Hermanos Penitentes, 10, 110; political organization of, 116
Lucero, Marcella, 82
LULAC. *See* League of United Latin
American Citizens

MALDEF. *See* Mexican American Legal Defense Foundation
males, Chicano, 42
Mariachi mass, 49–50
marriage, 48; intermarriage, 64
Marxism, 30
media, 96–97; participation in politics,
115
Medicaid, 37
medicine, Aztec, 73
Memmi, Albert, 84, 102

Mexican-American border, 20–21, 23–24, 124
Mexican American Legal Defense Foundation (MALDEF), 127
Mexican American War, 1–2
Mexican Revolution, 79
Mirande, Alfredo, 15, 48, 96
Montezuma, 75
multi-segmented social system, 42–44
murals, 111, 118
Murieta, Juaguin, 110
music, 96, 118
Myrdal, Gunner, 83, 102, 109

NACS. See National Association of Chicano Studies
National Association of Chicano Studies (NACS), 10, 129
National Council of La Rasa, 10, 129
Native Americans, 55–56; life expectancy of, 62
Nevada, 24
New Jersey, politics of, 121
New Mexico, 15, 24; politics of, 119, 121, 128; Santa Fe, 15
New York, 121
Nieto Gomez, Anna, 82
Nisbet, Robert, 4
norms, 92–97
Norwood, Robin, 52

Ohio, 124
oppression, ideological, national, and international, 139
organizations, political, 115
Orozco, Jose Clemente, 111

paradigms, 9, 15–16, 87–88; in the social sciences, 87
Paredes, Americo, 110
Paredes, Gregorio Cortez, 110
parole officers, 108
pecan shelling strike, 81
Penitente Brotherhood, 97, 110; Easter ritual, 56; political, cultural, Anglo domination, 124
Penitentiaries, 125
poetry, 118

police, 108
Political organization, 117
Politics, 106, 115–36, 139; electoral, non-electoral, 115–36; media and, 115; priests in, 132; state, 121–22
poverty, 139
priests, ministers, and religion, 132
psychology, 106
Puerto Ricans, 126; politics and, 124; women, 126

Quetzalcoatl, 74
quincinera (dances), 91

religion, 48
Republican Party, 124, 127
Republicans, 122, 127; administration, 124, 130
Rivera, Diego, 111
role models, for women, 79
Ryan, William, 14

Saiz, Flor, 73
scientists, 108
Siqueiros, David Alfaro, 111
social bandit, 110
social change, 140
social control, 92–97
social deviance, 92–97
social fact, 144
socialization, and the family, 146
social responsibility, for racism, 148
social sciences, 140–41
social stratification: in academe, 82; by class, by gender, by race, 30–31
social workers, 37
socioeconomic status, in a capitalistic structure, 30–39
sociology, 4–6, 13–17, 32, 36, 140–41; Chicano, 15; Emile Durkheim, 144; feminist, 73; of Mexican Americans, Chicanos, 9
Southwest Voter Registration Project, 126
Spanish language, 130–31
spirits, 49
suicide, 65

Talamantez, Inez, 82
teenagers, 64, 76. *See also* youth
Tenayuca, Emma, 81
Texas, 74–75, 101, 119; the Alamo, 109; annexation of, 23–24; G. I. Forum, 117; history, 20–21; Jose Angel Gutierrez, 119; La Llorona, 76; LULAC, 119; pecan shelling strike of 1938, 80; politics, 117, 121, 128; Raza Unida Party, 119; voting, 121
Texas Rangers, 110
Tijerina, Reis Lopes, 119–20
Treaty of Guadalupe Hidalgo, 1–2, 24
Trujillo, Marcella (Lucero), 82

United Farm Workers, 10
U.S. Bureau of the Census, Mexican American, Native Americans, and, 62
Utah, 24

Valasquez, Willie, 126, 132
Valazquez, Diana, 73–74
Vietnamese, 147
violence, 139

Virgin de Guadalupe, 49
voting, 115

war, 118
War on Poverty, 119
weddings, 91
women, 67–89; internal colonial model, feminists, 141; in politics, 135
women's studies, 109
Women's Vote Project, 126
workers, 37, 84; Anglo and Chicano, 103; and capitalism, 30, 37, 39; Cesar Chávez, 120; Chicana, 81; Bert Corona, organizing, 80; GOP, 124; and the middle class, 38; migrant, 124; poverty, 37; undocumented, 121, 131; United Farm Workers, 120; women, 87
working class, youth, 38
World War II, 116–17

Yberra, Lea, 82
youth: cholos, choloas, 106; leadership, in politics, and the future, 132–33

zoot suit riots, 80–81

About the Author

IRENE I. BLEA, born in the mountains of northern New Mexico, has a Ph.D. in sociology from the University of Colorado at Boulder. Currently she is an associate professor at Metropolitan State College in Denver, where she teaches Chicano studies in the department of sociology. Her areas of specialization are race-ethnic relations, qualitative theory and methods, and deviant behavior.

Prior to becoming an educator, Blea was a mental health therapist specializing in ethnotherapy and family therapy. She received a B.A. in sociology and an A.A. in mental health at the University of Southern Colorado at Pueblo. She was employed on the wards of the Colorado State Hospital, an institution for the mentally impaired, where she worked in one of the children's cottages, the alcoholic ward, and wards housing the mentally retarded.

Blea has an international reputation as a scholar and has several publications in Chicano studies and women's studies. She also is a poet with many publications and honors, including first place in the Martin Luther King, Jr., literary contest; the Golden Poet Award; and finalist in the Denver Classic. Her works in progress include a book of poetry titled *Damn, Sam, I Want to Share My Life but I Need to Live Alone* and a historical novel tentatively titled *Suzanna: A Woman of Honor.* Her next textbook will focus upon the lives of Mexican American women.